Old Testament Survey

POETRY AND PROPHECY

(JOB – MALACHI)

by

CLARENCE H. BENSON, LITT. D.

1972 Revision

EVANGELICAL TEACHER TRAINING ASSOCIATION
   Box 327
   Wheaton, Illinois 60187

Courses in the Preliminary Certificate Program

Old Testament Survey — Law and History
Old Testament Survey — Poetry and Prophecy
New Testament Survey
Understanding People
Understanding Teaching or Teaching Techniques
Sunday School Success

1972 Revision
Third Printing 1976

ISBN 0-910566-02-X

© 1961, 1962, 1963, 1972 by Evangelical Teacher Training Association
Printed in U.S.A.

CONTENTS

Introduction / 4

About Hebrew Poetry / 5

1. The Integrity of the Redeemed / 7
   Job

2. Songs of the Redeemed / 13
   Psalms (Part 1)

3. Themes of the Psalms / 19
   Psalms (Part 2)

4. Wisdom Literature / 26
   Proverbs, Ecclesiastes, Song of Solomon

5. Understanding the Prophetic Books / 33

6. The Great Messianic Prophet / 39
   Isaiah

7. Prophecies of Judgment upon Judah / 47
   Jeremiah and Lamentations

8. Prophecy of Restoration / 53
   Ezekiel

9. Great Prophecies of World Empires / 59
   Daniel

10. Hosea, Joel, Amos, Obadiah / 66

11. Jonah, Micah, Nahum, Habakkuk / 75

12. Zephaniah, Haggai, Zechariah, Malachi / 84

Chart — The Divided Kingdom Era / 93

Map — The Old Testament World / 94

Concerning E.T.T.A. / 95

A knowledge of the content of the whole Bible and ways of communicating truth are imperative if one is to understand God's revelation and to teach the people of God. For this reason, Evangelical Teacher Training Association provides courses of study in both Bible and Christian education in its program of leadership preparation.

Believers desiring a better understanding of the Word of God and sufficient background knowledge of the Old Testament to teach others will find this text, *Old Testament Survey - Poetry and Prophecy,* of immense help.

This is the second of two survey texts giving a sweeping overview of Old Testament content. The first, *Old Testament Survey - Law and History,* considers the first seventeen books of the Old Testament. Here, in easy-to-read form, is a survey of the interesting poetry and prophecy Bible books. It is a complete study in itself, carefully condensing and preserving the historical sequence of Old Testament events. The course is profitable for in-service training as well as initial survey study for prospective teacher preparation.

Those familiar with the former E.T.T.A. textbook on this subject will recognize the same basic content in this text — rearranged and clearly outlined. A map and chart are included at the end of the text and a bibliography is at the end of each chapter. Thought-provoking questions are provided to cause students to rethink and crystallize the major truths presented. Thus they are encouraged to participate in discovering and interpreting Bible truths for daily living. Instead of a summarizing paragraph at the end of each chapter, the student will find an excellent summary-review by rereading the portions underlined in color.

Proper study of this text will eventuate in more than intellectual pursuit and accumulation of factual knowledge. "What does the Word say to me?" must be the constant self-interrogation of the student. A determined effort to apply the teaching of the Word to current living will result in rewarding experience.

PAUL E. LOTH, ED.D., *President*
Evangelical Teacher Training Association

The Hebrew language, because of its inherent emotional qualities, lends itself effectively to poetic expression. Abstract ideas can be indicated in concrete, sensuous, image-bearing Hebrew terms. The Psalms illustrate this when they speak of God's power as "His hands," or the approach to death as "the valley of the shadow."

Poetry has been described as "the form of literature which embodies beautiful thought, feeling, or action in rhythmical and unusually metrical language." Whether rhyming or non-rhyming, poetry must have rhythm or meter. The few instances of rhyme in the Old Testament are too insufficient to be certain that they were done purposefully.

Parallelism, a special kind of meter, is a distinguishing feature of Hebrew poetry. Each poetic line of Hebrew must have at least two parts — a balance between thought and ideas. Because of this fact, Hebrew poetry loses less beauty in translation than other language forms.

Each simple verse will have two stichs, or two parts, in which each word in the first stich will correspond to a word in the second stich as in Isaiah 1:3 — "Israel doth not know; my people doth not consider."

There are six distinct types of parallelism to be found in Hebrew poetry:

Synonymous — both parts means the same, as in Psalm 15:1; 24:3; 114.

Antithetic — two parts presenting a contrast, as in Psalm 1:6; Proverbs 1:29; 10:1, 7.

Synthetic — adding of information, such as the second part adding to the first and moving on, as in Psalm 1:3; Proverbs 3:5, 6, 7.

Emblematic — involving a literal statement in one part, which is supported by a metaphor in the other, as in Psalm 42:1.

Stairlike (Climactic) — some of the first part is repeated, which is further developed in the second, as in Psalm 29:1, 2a; 94:3; 95:1-3; 121:1, 2, 3, 4.

Introverted — arrangement of four parts so that the first is a parallel with the fourth, and the second with the third, as in Psalm 123:1, 2; Proverbs 23:15, 16.

Generally, Hebrew poetry is either lyric or didactic. Lyrical poetry can be put to music and is intended for singing; didactical poetry instructs.

Among the poetical books, the Psalms, Song of Solomon, and Lamentations are lyrical poetry, while Proverbs and Ecclesiastes are didactical.

JOHN H. STOLL, PH.D.

THE INTEGRITY OF THE REDEEMED

1

Job

The Old Testament is divided into three divisions: historical (Genesis - Esther), poetical (Job - Song of Solomon), prophetical (Isaiah-Malachi). Approximately the same number of chapters are devoted to each division. The book of Job begins the poetical section.

The poetical books are thus called because they are composed almost entirely of Hebrew verse. The poetical element, however, is not limited to the five poetical books. Almost every part of the Bible contains poetry. Large portions of its prose, especially in the prophetic books, rise by noble thoughts and beautiful sentiments into the sphere of genuine poetry.

Chronologically the book of Job belongs to the period of Genesis. Tradition ascribes the book to Moses. indicating it was written during his stay in Midian. If this is correct, Job is the oldest book in the Bible, even preceding the writing of the book of Genesis.

The last of the historical books, Esther, and the first of the poetical, Job, have much in common. They present two eastern princes, Ahasuerus and Job, in the hands of God and Satan. Job is considered to be the greatest man, and Ahasuerus the greatest king in the East. Both books exhibit God's constant care. In the one case, a beloved man; in the other, a cherished nation. Both books show Satan's hostility to individuals and nations. In both books God is glorified, Satan is defeated, and man is blessed.

ABOUT THE BOOK OF JOB

The subject of the book of Job is not the conversion of a sinner, but the consecration of a saint. The theme of the book is the study of affliction.

Studies in Nature

No other book in the Bible contains as much natural theology. The characters presented facts in astronomy which have not been generally known until recent days. Their knowledge of physical geography and zoology was most accurate. One of the oldest books in the world, the book of Job refers to the rotundity of the earth; the suspension of the earth in space; the circular motion and density of the clouds; the names of present-day stars and constellations; the rotation and the revolution of the earth.[1]

Study of Satan

The book of Job is unusual in its study of Satan. No other book reveals such information about the "prince of this world." God disclosed the fact that the adversary is a person; that he has great power; that he controls the winds and lightning of heaven, and plagues and diseases of earth. He is the "accuser of the brethren." But while he is the author of all evil, he cannot tempt man without God's permission.[2] Satan is presented in his role as an accuser of the brethren. When God calls his attention to the righteousness of Job, whom Satan had been unable to corrupt, Satan charges Job with a mercenary spirit and declares that if God took away Job's temporal blessings, he would no longer be loyal to Him. God accepts Satan's challenge, not so much that Job's loyalty might be tested, as that the power of God's grace to keep His servant might be demonstrated.

THE TIME OF JOB

It is possible to determine with some degree of accuracy the time in which Job lived. He was one of the patriarchs, living probably before Abraham. At the time of his trial, he was married and had grown sons and daughters, the former living in homes of their own.

Early marriages were not common among the patriarchs. Isaac was forty years of age and Jacob eighty-four. Job may have been approximately sixty years old when the scene opens in the first chapter. Since he lived 140 years after this testing,[3] he must have been at least 200 years old when he died. As the longevity of the human race underwent a gradual decline after the Deluge until the Exodus, a study of Bible genealogy in Genesis 11 indicates that the period of Job could not consistently be placed later than Terah, the father of Abraham.

Some suggest that Job lived between the building of the Tower of Babel and the call of Abraham. The absence of any reference to the children of Israel and their laws, which is found in every other book of the Old Testament, and the failure to mention the Sodom and Gomorrah catastrophe while referring to the Deluge, would suggest a period prior to Abraham. Moreover, the religion of Job was the religion of the patriarchs, when the medium between God and man was the family altar and not the officiating priest of the Mosaic dispensation.

THE MAN JOB (Chapters 1 — 2)

Job is the principal speaker and character in the book. It is significant that the name in Hebrew means *the one persecuted* or *the one who turns to God.*

There is little ground for questioning Job as a historical character. In Ezekiel 14, he is mentioned with Noah and Daniel, as one of the three great intercessors in whom God delighted. In the New Testament, James refers to both Job and Elijah in chapter 5. If one is recognized as a historical character, the other must be also.

If Job were only a mythological character, such implication would be given either in the book itself or in references to it. Christ plainly designated His parables as such, and no other method of discernment between fact and fiction in Scriptures would be worthy of the Word of God. All the other great poems in the Bible, such as the song of Moses in Exodus 15 and the song of Deborah in Judges 5, are based entirely upon historical incidents.

Job was Wealthy

Job was one of the wealthiest men in the East and may have been the greatest of his time. He had great herds of cattle and a retinue of servants, which constituted the wealth of that time. He knew the benefits of an established civilization, for he had a fixed residence. He lived in a house in a city[4] and not in a tent as did Abraham and Jacob.

Job was Respected

Job was great in reputation as well as in possessions. He sat as a chief and dwelt like a king in the city. Young and old showed him deference. Princes and nobles honored him. He was father to the poor and judge to the oppressed.

Job was Righteous

Job was pleasing to God as well as to men. Despite the idolatry all about him, he was faithful in worshiping the one true God. He offered sacrifices for himself and his children daily. He loved righteousness and hated evil. In chapter one he was commended as a "perfect" man. That perfection indicated completeness of character and uprightness in thought and action. Job's life was not perfect in the sense of holiness, as he himself admitted. His confession of the need of a Redeemer is the climactic utterance of the book.[5]

JOB'S TRIAL (Chapters 3 — 37)

Job's loyalty to God was put to a severe test. God *tried* him, but Satan *tempted* him. Each calamity was followed by another. He lost his oxen and his asses, then his sheep, then his camels, and finally his sons and daughters. The words, "while he was yet speaking," repeated three times show the rapidity and vehemence of Satan's attacks. Still Job remained true to God. He knew that God had given him all that he possessed and that it was God's right to take it from him.

But Satan was not satisfied. He requested permission to test Job's integrity by the affliction of a loathsome disease. Job became a pitiable object, so repulsive that even his wife and relatives deserted him. Yet he steadfastly refused to renounce his faith in God. His persistent faith under trial proved that he did not serve God for wealth, family, or health.

Visit of Eliphaz, Bildad, and Zophar (Chapters 3 — 31)

The most severe trial of all occurred when three friends — Eliphaz, Bildad, and Zophar — came to sympathize, but stayed to criticize. In reality they voiced the trouble that Job so much feared. They intimated that the religious world would believe that Job was a hypocrite, a secretly wicked man, because of the overwhelming calamities which had befallen him. Their speeches and Job's replies occupy a large portion of the book. Their philosophy was poured upon the afflicted man in three rounds of speeches, to each of which Job replied in self-defense.

Eliphaz represented the man of science. He argued from experience and from facts. He satisfied himself that Job was undoubtedly a secret sinner. Bildad's arguments were based on tradition. His address was shorter and his language was rougher than that of Eliphaz.

Zophar was a moralist. He believed in salvation by self-merit and endeavored to prove that Job's calamities were the result of his sins of omission.

In the second and third round of speeches the philosophers were more vehement in their assertions of Job's guilt and less considerate of his pitiable condition. In fact, the more they argued, the less they accomplished. Job spoke of them as "miserable comforters" who had little comprehension of his sufferings. Then he left them and turned to God, pouring out his soul in lamentation and maintaining his innocence of their insinuations.

Address of Elihu (Chapters 32 — 37)

While the addresses of Eliphaz, Bildad, and Zophar were in progress, there was an attentive listener whose youth and inexperience did not permit him to join in the debate. Young as he was, Elihu discovered that wisdom is not necessarily the possession of seniors and scholars. When Eliphaz, Bildad, and Zophar could not convince Job that his suffering was the result of sin, Elihu came forward and presented a new argument. He condemned the three friends because they unjustly accused Job of hypocrisy, and Job because he charged God with injustice. He admonished all of them to witness God's greatness in creation and His goodness in revelation.

Elihu was the "daysman" whom Job desired[6], for Elihu argued that affliction could have educative value, and that God had ultimate good in store for the sufferer. He pointed out that there was no moral difference between Job and his three accusers — that all were sinners and alike needed a Savior. He thus disclosed the foundation doctrines of the New Testament.

ADMONITION OF GOD (Chapters 38 — 41)

Job had complained that God kept silent and would not attend to his lamentations, but after the address of Elihu, the answer came. In these chapters, one of the most sublime portions of Scripture, God addresses Job, and His theme is Himself. Elihu had presented the wisdom and the power of God. Now God reveals Himself.

It is notable that Jehovah gives no explanation of Job's sufferings, renders no decision on the subject in debate, and offers no hint of compensation to His servant for what he had endured. He showed that His dealing with Job was beyond criticism.

RESTORATION OF JOB (Chapter 42)

As a result of this manifestation of God, Job abhorred himself. He was then directed to offer prayer for his three friends, and in so doing was vindicated in their eyes. Thus Job, like Noah and Daniel, became a great intercessor. Not only was he vindicated, but he lived long enough to see children and grandchildren, to double his former fortune, and to regain his prior prestige and prosperity.

Why must God's children suffer? It may be for discipline, for spiritual development, or above all else, for the glory of God. God's purpose in using Satan is to develop character through trial and to make men partakers of His holiness. We must always remember that it was not so much a question of Job's loyalty as it was of God's power. "God is faithful."

Job's example has provided comfort and courage to the afflicted in all ages. But the One who suffered greatest affliction was not Job, but Jesus Christ. He is the answer to Job's question, "If a man die, shall he live *again*?" He, and not Elihu, fully supplied Job's longing for someone to stand between him and God. The Lord Jesus Christ is our Mediator.

NOTES

[1] Job 22:14; 26:7; 28:24-26; 38:31, 32
[2] I Corinthians 10:13
[3] Job 42:16
[4] Job 1:4; 29:7
[5] Job 19:25
[6] Job 9:33

FOR REVIEW AND DISCUSSION

1. What is the theme of the book of Job?
2. Characterize the man Job.
3. State briefly and evaluate the philosophies of Job's friends.
4. Discuss how we may learn to respond to suffering as illustrated by Job.
5. Compare and contrast the sufferings of Job and Christ.

FOR ADDITIONAL ENRICHMENT

BARNES, ALBERT. *Job*. Notes on the Old Testament. Grand Rapids: Baker Book House, 1950.

MACKINTOSH, C. H. *Job and His Friends*. Miscellaneous Writings, vol. 1. New York: Loizeaux Bros., 10th prtg. 1960.

MORGAN, G. CAMPBELL. *The Book of Job*. Westwood, N.J.: Fleming H. Revell Co., 1909.

RIDOUT, SAMUEL. *The Book of Job*. New York: Loizeaux Bros., 4th prtg. 1958.

YODER, S. C. *Poetry of the Old Testament*. Scottdale, Pa.: Herald Press, reprint 1952.

SONGS OF THE REDEEMED 2

Psalms (Part 1)

The book of Psalms is a connecting link between the Old and the New Testaments. In it, the great purposes and lessons of the Mosaic law are expressed. In the Psalms, the Hebrews were taught that the form of the law without the spirit was vain, and that a spiritual God required spiritual worship. Moreover, the mind of the worshiper was concentrated on the Messiah, whose presence and power were to dominate the New Testament.

No other book in the Bible more truly magnifies the Word of God. Psalm 119 contains glowing tributes to the Scriptures in 174 of its 176 verses. Many Psalms reiterate a loyal devotion to the sacred Word, as well as a holy and happy contemplation of it. The Psalms contain sufficient evidence to prove the inspiration of the Scriptures independent of all other sources. They are quoted or clearly referred to in the New Testament almost seventy times, thus taking first place among the Old Testament books quoted by New Testament writers.

THE PURPOSE OF THE PSALMS

The book of Psalms, even as Job, was written more for the saint than for the sinner. It is composed of songs for the redeemed, rather than of messages for the unbeliever.

Written to be Sung

The Psalms were designed for vocal expression and instrumental accompaniment. For the most part Hebrew poetry is lyrical, a name given to it because it was originally accompanied by music of the lyre.

One word translated "psalm" means a *composition set to music*. The musicians of Israel were not paid. Certain families possessing natural talent contributed their service generation after generation for congregational worship.

The Hebrews used a wide range of instruments. Many musical instruments were used in the worship service by the choirs in the temple. In the grand hallelujah chorus of Psalm 150, no less than eight different instruments are mentioned.

Instruments seemed to have three classifications. The first group was composed of *wind instruments*. The shofar, or ram's horn, is called "trumpet" in the first line of Psalm 150:3. This is not the cornet, which is recorded as a distinct instrument. A third wind instrument is rendered "pipe" in the Revised Version, which is better than "organ," as the keyboard was not invented until centuries later.

To the second group belonged the *stringed instruments*. The harp was most frequently mentioned and there were several varieties. The triangular harp with four strings was known as the sackbut.[1] The Psaltery sometimes embraced a whole class of stringed instruments similar to those in modern use.

The third group contained the *percussion instruments*. The timbrel was a sort of tambourine which was drummed with the fingers. The several kinds of cymbals were used to keep rhythm.[2]

Used by the Early Church

The Psalms may be the hymns that the Lord and His disciples sang[3] and that constituted the hymnology of the early Church. Peter on the Day of Pentecost referred to David's psalm[4] and Paul at Antioch quoted from the Psalms as Scripture.[5]

The book of Psalms was the hymnbook of Israel that has provided much source material for the music of the church. Paul and Silas praised God with Psalms in the prison at midnight. The great missionary apostle exhorted the Christians at Ephesus and Colosse to teach and admonish one another with Psalms.[6]

Related to Today's Living

The Psalms are models of acceptable devotion. Other parts of revelation represent God as speaking to man; here man is represented as speaking to God. By this book we can test the utterances and feelings of our hearts and learn whether our prayer and our praise are expressed in a manner acceptable to God. Prayers that contain the language of this divine poety, and songs that convey the words and the message of these inspired writings, are devotional utterances pleasing to God.

The Psalms are models of ethical expression. Morality has its roots in both the Old Testament and the New. Man's relation to God determines the rightness or wrongness of his relation to his fellow-men. The Psalms make a clear distinction between sin and righteousness, the wicked and the righteous. The words "righteous" and "righteousness" occur more than 130 times in the 150 chapters. The words "sin" and "iniquity" are found sixty-five times, and "good" and "evil" about forty times. These words embody rich ethical and religious concepts and imply a standard of human conduct which is consistent with the revelation of His divine character — His holiness, power, wisdom, love, and grace.

For Spiritual Encouragement

Psalms 1 and 23 probably are the most familiar. The opening Psalm exalts the Word of God and contrasts the present and the future state of the godly and ungodly. The Shepherd Psalm exalts the providence of God. It is, with the possible exception of the Lord's Prayer, the best known portion of Scripture. It has been the favorite Psalm of multitudes of Christians and has inspired new confidence and courage in the divine Shepherd. It has pillowed many a soul passing through the valley of death. After the Shepherd Psalm, perhaps Psalm 103 which eulogizes the loving kindness of God is the general favorite.

Six of the Psalms are morning hymns and three are evening songs. Four begin with the words, "O give thanks." Psalm 65 is the farmer's song; Psalm 104, creation's story; Psalm 121, the traveler's prayer; Psalm 148, nature's hallelujah. The shortest chapter in the Bible is Psalm 117; it is also the middle chapter. The longest is Psalm 119. In Psalm 136, each of its twenty-six verses ends with the phrase, "for His mercy endureth forever."

ARRANGEMENT OF THE PSALMS

The Psalter, like the Pentateuch, is arranged in five historically significant books or divisions. The greater number of Psalms cluster around three periods of Hebrew history — the reign of David and Solomon, the reign of Hezekiah, and the period of the captivity and return. The Psalms of the earlier period of the kingdom are in the first book; those relating to the later kingdom period, in the second and third books. The exilic and post-exilic Psalms are for the most part in the fourth and fifth books. It is probable that the first book was compiled by David, the second by Solomon, the third by "the men of Hezekiah," and the fourth and fifth by Ezra and Nehemiah.[7]

A doxology concludes each book and clearly marks its separation from the one following. Like the Sermon on the Mount, the Psalms begin with a beatitude and appropriately rise to a grand finale of praise in the group known as the Hallelujah Psalms, the concluding composition being a hallelujah chorus.

AUTHORSHIP OF THE PSALMS

The Psalms were collected over a period of a thousand years, the contribution of more than a dozen writers. The period of their composition extends from about 1400 B.C., when Moses wrote Psalm 90, until 444 B.C., when Ezra completed the canon and, according to the Septuagint, added Psalms 1 and 119. Despite the wide separation of time and station between the composers, there is marvelous unity of thought and spirit. This can only be explained by divine authorship.

At least seventy-three Psalms were written by David, and two by Solomon. This accounts for almost one-half of the Psalms. Twelve are ascribed to Asaph, the Levite director of David's choir, and twelve to the Korah family of singers. Most of Asaph's Psalms indicate a later date than David's time and were probably written by his descendants who were designated for Temple service.[8] Heman and Ethan[9], court musicians, are each credited with one Psalm. The Septuagint ascribes three to Isaiah, two to Jeremiah, and the final three to Haggai and Zechariah.

Forty-eight of the Psalms are anonymous. This is almost one-third of the Psalms. In many instances, however, it has been possible to locate the author. Acts 4:25 and Hebrews 4:7 reveal the fact that David wrote both Psalm 2 and Psalm 95. "Selah," which some have interpreted to mean *pause*, at the close of Psalm 9 which was written by David, may suggest that the one following was also from his pen. If Hezekiah's songs[10] were ever incorporated in the Psalter, they may be the ten anonymous Songs of Degrees, one for each of the retraced degrees on the sun dial of Ahaz,[11] and five, by two other authors, added to make up the number of years of life which were granted to Hezekiah after his sickness.

Many of the writers of the Psalms were musicians who composed both the words and the music of the selection. The musical setting of these hymns is better understood with a knowledge of the Levitical organization of orchestra and chorus.

Many of the immortal poems of the Old Testament were prompted by some great national crisis which touched the heartstrings of the people. The song of Moses was inspired by the tragedy of the Red Sea;[12] the song of Deborah by the defeat of the Canaanites and the bold assassination of Sisera.[13] The crises in David's life were the inspiration for many Psalms. Other poems were the outburst of praise and thanksgiving for some remarkable deliverance or other extraordinary experience.

SUPERSCRIPTIONS OF THE PSALMS

One hundred and sixteen of the Psalms have titles. These titles are not a part of the sacred text, but are highly instructive as to the circumstances which led to the composition of the Psalms, name of the author, directions to the musician, the historical occasion, the liturgical use, the style of the poet, the accompanying instrument, the rhythm to which the words are to be sung. Sometimes all of these are combined, as in Psalm 60. Thorough study of these distinctions will enrich the Christian's life even though the inspiration of the superscriptions cannot be supported. They presumably were added in Ezra's time at the close of the Old Testament.

THE MESSAGE OF THE PSALMS

Revealed Theology

No other Old Testament book teaches as much about God. The theological outline includes omnipotence, omniscience, omnipresence, eternity, and immutability. God's natural and moral attributes are frequently set forth.

Natural Theology

Only the book of Job surpasses the Psalms in natural theology. The psalmist uses nature to demonstate God as a marvelous and mighty creator as well as a provider and protector. Many allusions in this book illuminate the prehistoric pages of creation and suggest scientific information far in advance of the prevailing knowledge of that early time. Many natural scenes are painted with artistic effect, like the storm at sea;[14] the pastoral pictures;[15] the starry heavens.[16]

Prophecy

The Psalms abound in prophecy. They contain predictions of the history of Christ and describe with wonderful accuracy His sufferings and glory. Christ calls attention to this fact in Luke 24:44. The book of Psalms is the Gospel in prophecy. There is no better proof of the inspiration of Scriptures than the drama of our Lord's crucifixion, as depicted in the Psalms a thousand years before He was born. The Gospels record what Christ said and did, and what was said and done to Him. The Psalms reveal His inner life — how He felt, and how He lived in the presence of His God and Father.

There are also chapters setting forth the future history of Israel and the millennial glory of Jerusalem.

NOTES

[1] Daniel 3:5
[2] I Chronicles 15:19
[3] Matthew 26:30
[4] Acts 1:16; Psalm 41:9
[5] Acts 13:29-34
[6] Ephesians 5:19; Colossians 3:16
[7] Proverbs 25:1; II Chronicles 29:30
[8] I Chronicles 25:1, 2
[9] I Chronicles 15:16, 17
[10] Isaiah 38:20
[11] Isaiah 38:8
[12] Exodus 15
[13] Judges 5
[14] Psalm 107:25-30
[15] Psalms 65; 104
[16] Psalms 8; 19

FOR REVIEW AND DISCUSSION

1. How does the book of Psalms magnify the Word of God?
2. Illustrate four important uses of the Psalms.
3. How does each of the five books, or divisions, of the Psalms close?
4. What proof is there that many of the Psalms were inspired by some extraordinary experience?
5. Explain the value of the titles of the Psalms.

FOR ADDITIONAL ENRICHMENT

ARCHER, GLEASON L., JR. A Survey of Old Testament Introduction. Chicago: Moody Press. 1964.

HARRIS, R. LAIRD. "Psalms," The Biblical Expositor, vol. II. Edited by Carl F. Henry. Philadelphia: A. J. Holman Co., 1960.

SCROGGIE, W. GRAHAM. The Psalms. New York: Fleming H. Revell Co., 1965.

SPURGEON, C. H. Treasury of David. 3 vols. Grand Rapids: Zondervan Publishing House, 1957.

THEMES OF THE PSALMS   3

Psalms (*Part 2*)

This ancient collection of hymns of praise and worship can be classified under many general themes. Some Psalms deal with several different, yet related themes. Psalm 19, for instance, extols both the works and the words of God. It might therefore be listed either as a Psalm of nature or a Psalm of precept. The classification of some of the Psalms is largely arbitrary and rests on the decision of the individual.

Of all the various classifications six are most prominent and account for the major framework of the Psalms. These are:

Penitential Psalms which ask God's forgiveness, such as 32, 38, 51.

Acrostic Psalms which have verses or sections of the Psalm beginning with succeeding Hebrew alphabetic letters, such as 25, 119 (complete), 145 (partial).

Hallelujah Psalms which praise Jehovah. The word "hallelujah" means *praise the Lord*, such as 146 – 150.

Imprecatory Psalms which reveal the vindictive attitude of the psalmist toward his enemies and also call down a curse, such as 35, 69, 109.

Historical Psalms which present important historical events in poetic form, such as 78, 105, 114.

Prophetical Psalms which tell of coming events. Especially prominent in this class are the Messianic Psalms which look forward to the coming and eventual reign of Christ, such as 22, 69, 110.

Only three of the classifications will be considered.

THE IMPRECATORY PSALMS

The imprecatory Psalms have greatly perplexed earnest-minded Christians, especially in the light of New Testament teaching regarding love for enemies.[1] Bible critics often quote such passages as Psalms 58:6; 109:10; 137:8, 9, as utterances of vindictive passion, and say that these could not have been written under the inspiration of the Holy Spirit.

It is well to keep in mind that the Bible, while free from error, often records what others said — evil men, good men, inspired men, and uninspired men. In the Psalms we have a record of what God said to man, and that is always true. On the other hand, there are many statements made by men, and these may or may not be true. The passages cited above are what men said to God, the inspired record of men's prayers to God. To God they breathed out the agony of their hearts, and to God they cried for vengeance on their enemies.

Is an expression of righteous indignation ever justifiable? Would either Old Testament or New Testament teaching allow it? Psalm 52 suggests an answer. Here is an outburst of David's indignation against the awful crime of Doeg. When King Saul's footmen refused to kill eighty-five Israelite priests who were falsely accused, Doeg, an Edomite herdsman, consented and ruthlessly slew with his cruel, murderous sword, not only the innocent priests, but men, women, children, oxen, asses, and sheep! The very mention of such atrocity stirs up feelings which cannot be suppressed. Such an expression of indignation was not to gratify personal malice nor was it private revenge.

When the psalmist called upon God to take vengeance on the wicked, he may have been anticipating the teaching of the New Testament. Vengeance belongs to God, He will repay. Instead of taking vengeance into his own hands, David was asking his righteous God to judge iniquity. There is certainly nothing wrong in praying God to break the teeth of wicked men who are using those teeth to tear the upright. Moreover, nothing was more conspicuous in the life of David than his generous and gracious dealings with his enemies. He not only refused to kill his bitterest and most relentless enemy, but prevented others from doing so.[2] Although David prayed, "Let his children be continually vagabonds and beg,"[3] he graciously sought out the grandson of his arch-enemy, Saul, and had him eat at the king's table as one of his own sons.[4]

The language of the Hebrew people is direct and concrete, not abstract. Where we speak of crime, they designate the criminal. The

Christian, on the other hand is taught to have compassion on the sinner, but to abhor his sin. Where the language makes no distinction between sin and sinner, directness of criticism is more readily seen.

THE HISTORICAL PSALMS

No portion of this book is more closely related to the rest of the Old Testament than the historical Psalms. Psalms 78, 105, and 106 are outstanding for their didactic use of history, but a historical strand is woven into the texture of the whole Psalter. Attempts have been made to connect all Psalms with some historical event, though many can be made applicable to various purposes. About twenty-one Psalms definitely refer to the history of Israel from the time of Moses to the days of the restoration. These historical allusions may be divided into three periods.

Period of the Theocracy

Compare the exodus, the wilderness wanderings, the settlement in Canaan, and the time of the judges as mentioned in Psalms 78:12-66; 105:23-45; 106:7-33; 114; 135:10, 11.

Period of the Kingdom

Many of David's Psalms are related to some personal crisis or experience. During the days of his persistent persecution by Saul, when his life was in constant jeopardy, David composed Psalms 7, 11, 34, 54. His coming to the throne and establishing national worship in Jerusalem gave rise to Psalm 24. The dedication of his house in peace after years of war and wandering was the occasion of Psalm 30. The shame of David's great sin and his genuine repentance produced the heart-stirring penitential prayers recorded in Psalm 51 and Psalm 32. The terrible consequences of his sin as manifested in Absalom's rebellion led him to compose Psalms 3, 4, 55. Only Psalm 60 appears to mark David's military triumphs. Psalm 18 and II Samuel 22 give a brief résumé of his life's experiences, and make reference to his victories over God's enemies.

One Psalm at least is credited to the disaster that befell Sennacherib's army. The anonymous Songs of Degrees, Psalms 120 – 134, can be associated with the sign given of Hezekiah's recovery in Isaiah 38. Some of these, such as Psalms 124, 126, 129, 130, suggest the Babylonian capitivity.

Period of the Province

The fall of Jerusalem and the profaning and burning of the Temple by Nebuchadnezzar are vividly described in Psalms 74 and 79. The sad lot of the exiles in Babylon is pictured in Psalms 80 and 137. The great joy of the returning captives is expressed in Psalms 85 and 126. At the time of the building and dedication of the second Temple, Haggai and Zechariah undoubtedly prepared Psalms 146, 147, and 150.

Without the Psalter, the recorded religious history of Israel would be imperfect and misleading. The Psalms bathe the black and forbidden rock of Israel's history in the sunlight of religious devotion and spiritual fervor. From these heart-throbbing hymns of experiences we perceive the true spirit of the circumstances which gave them rise.

THE PROPHETICAL PSALMS

No study is more fascinating than the prophetical Psalms. As the historical Psalms bind the Psalter to the remainder of the Old Testament, so the prophetical Psalms provide a connecting link with the New Testament.

Messianic

Much of Israel's future history, as well as the destiny of the Gentile nations, is revealed in the Psalms. The Messianic Psalms dominate the prophetic portions of the book. Psalm 40:6-10 is a distinct reference to the coming and mission of Jesus Christ. Psalms 41 and 109 picture the betrayal of Christ. Although Ahithophil was the traitor who partially fulfilled David's prediction in Psalm 41, this passage also applies to Judas. This is proved by Christ's quoting it on the night of His betrayal.[5] That Judas is designated in Psalm 109 is revealed by Peter at the election of Matthias.[6]

Humilation

At least two Psalms foretell the crucifixion of Christ. Psalm 22 is a graphic picture of death by crucifixion and the circumstances that were precisely fulfilled at Calvary. The fact that the Jewish form of capital punishment was by stoning and that crucifixion was unknown in David's time is strong proof of inspiration. Psalm 22 contains the exact words Christ on the cross uttered one thousand years later. It describes in detail the terrible suffering to which He would be subjected. Psalm 69 gives certain details that are not mentioned in the earlier Psalm. Passages from both Psalms are quoted by the Gospel writers.[7]

Coronation

Psalm 16 is the great Easter announcement of the Old Testament. It discloses the empty tomb of resurrection morning. Peter, on the Day of Pentecost, shows that the risen Lord is here predicted. Paul, preaching at Antioch, also calls attention to this prophecy of the resurrection.[8]

Psalms 89 and 132 predict that the Messiah shall come from the royal line of David. Peter applied these passages to Christ and not to Solomon.[9] Christ Himself calls attention to Psalm 118, where He is pictured as the chief Cornerstone.[10] The Messianic significance of this passage lies in the fact that it is quoted six times by New Testament writers, who relate it to Christ's rejection by the Jews.

Kingdom

Three Psalms portray the millennial reign of the Lord Jesus Christ. Psalm 2 foretells the rebellion of the nations against all law and authority just prior to the coming of Christ to establish His kingdom. Psalm 72 is a glorious description of Messiah's rule when "He shall have dominion also from sea to sea, and from the river unto the ends of the earth." Though certain passages may be applied to the golden age of Solomon, such a prediction as, "His name shall endure forever," clearly points to a greater than Solomon. Every verse in Psalm 110 refers to Christ's priestly Kingship.

Psalm 8 presents the most complete vision of Messiah. It traces the four stages of His marvelous career as man. The passage, "Thou hast made Him a little lower than the angels," refers to His earthly birth and life of rejection. "Thou hast crowned Him with glory and honor," describes His resurrection, ascension, and exaltation at the right hand of God. "Thou madest Him to have dominion over the work of Thy hands," predicts His millennial reign on earth. "Thou hast put all things under His feet," looks forward to His eternal reign.

Psalms 22, 23, and 24 may be taken together as a trilogy to view the past, present, and future of our Lord's work. These are sometimes called the Psalms of the cross, the crook, and the crown. They represent Christ's ministry as Savior, Shepherd, and Sovereign.

Israel

Both Israel and Jerusalem are the subjects of nearly a dozen Psalms, the most interesting of which is Psalm 102, "The Psalm of the Wandering Jew." The dispersion of Israel began with the captivity of the ten tribes by Assyria. Judah and Benjamin followed into Babylon, and only a comparatively small number returned under Zerubbabel and Ezra. The final dispersion by Rome in A.D. 70 sealed the doom of Jerusalem and started the last remnant on its long journey. The psalmist draws the future picture of his wandering people as one clothed in a garment of sackcloth, and casting dust and ashes upon his head as the signs of his sorrow.

Although Israel's sun seems to have set, the psalmist cannot believe it is forever. He has faith in God and looks for a miraculous resurrection of his nation. Thus in the latter part of the Psalm, hope succeeds bitter lamentations. God will again look with favor upon Israel as a nation and rebuild the beloved city of Jerusalem. Today, after all these years of desolation, the wandering Jew still regards the old city with great affection, even as the psalmist did. Equally significant and startling, in view of the present revival of Palestine and return of the Jew, is the prediction, "When the Lord shall build up Zion, He shall appear in His glory."[11]

The Psalms were well adapted as an expression of Israel's praise for the providential manifestation of God's interest in His chosen people. They are equally appropriate today to express the Christian's prayer and praise and are most valuable for spiritual enrichment. It is difficult to sing or read the Psalms without having our hearts enlarged, our affections purified, and our thoughts drawn heavenward.

Other books like the Pentateuch and Prophets may furnish much material for theological doctrine and for right principles of worship, but this book is a rich source of religious experience. Luther called it "a small Bible," and declared that there never could be a more precious book of examples and records of saints than the Psalter.

NOTES

[1] Matthew 5:44
[2] I Samuel 26:5-9
[3] Psalm 109:10
[4] II Samuel 9:1, 2, 11
[5] John 13:18
[6] Acts 1:20
[7] Matthew 27:34, 35; John 19:24, 29
[8] Acts 13:34-37

9 Acts 2:30
10 Matthew 21:42
11 Psalm 102:16

FOR REVIEW AND DISCUSSION

1. Name six prominent classifications of the Psalms.
2. How could the imprecatory Psalms be justified?
3. What is the basis for calling a Psalm a historic Psalm?
4. State several facts of Christ's life depicted in the Messianic Psalms.
5. What three successive Psalms portray Christ's ministry?

FOR ADDITIONAL ENRICHMENT

See chapter 2, page 18.

WISDOM LITERATURE

4

Proverbs, Ecclesiastes, Song of Solomon

The contents of Proverbs, Ecclesiastes, and Song of Solomon were collected, if not compiled, by Solomon, the renowned king of Israel. The three books are spoken of as the Wisdom Literature of the ancient Hebrew people who suggested that the Song of Solomon was composed during Solomon's youth, Proverbs during his manhood, and Ecclesiastes in his old age. Bible scholars differ in attributing all of these to Solomonic authorship.

Proverbs — **Poems on Practical Piety**

The Hebrew word translated "proverb" literally signifies *likeness* or *comparison*. Originally it involved the idea of a simile, but later it was given a wider significance. It came to denote such short pointed sayings that do not involve direct comparison, but convey their meaning by the help of a figure. From this stage it passed to sententious maxims generally, many of which involved a comparison. This form of instruction became popular among Eastern people. The majority of the population were not acquainted with the art of writing, and manuscripts were few. Great truths stated in concise comparisons strengthened the oral teaching of that day. These trenchant sayings were generally memorized, and the ability to repeat them was recognized as an evidence of religious education.

What the book of Psalms is to the devotional life, Proverbs is to the practical life. The Psalms warm the heart toward God in holy and pious affection. The Proverbs make the face shine before men in prudent, discreet, honest, and useful living. In the Psalms, love to God is exhibited; in Proverbs, it is love to our neighbor. As a collection of moral precepts for the regulation of fathers, mothers, children, and servants in families; of kings, magistrates, and civilians in states; Proverbs contains more true practical wisdom than all the philosophies of Greece and Rome. It goes beyond what modern writers have been able to produce.

Christ in His teaching employed proverbs such as "Physician, heal theyself;"[1] "A prophet is not without honor, save in his own country."[2]

AUTHORSHIP

Solomon composed at least three thousand proverbs,[3] but only a portion of them have been preserved. Wise and instructive as these proverbs may have been, it is no surprise that some of them are omitted from the inspired record, for John 20:30 declares that even in the case of "a greater than Solomon" many miracles were wrought which were not specifically recorded.

KEYNOTE VERSE

The keynote of the book of Proverbs is, "The fear of the Lord is the beginning of wisdom,"[4] a saying so true and fundamental that it ought to be engraved over the entrance of every institution of learning. It should be in the heart of every teacher. The word "fear" means *godly reverence*. It is mentioned fourteen times in Proverbs. This sentiment is also found in Job 28:28 and Psalm 111:10.

DIVISIONS OF THE BOOK

There are five natural divisions of the book of Proverbs. The first nine chapters contain various instructions and incentives to the study of true wisdom. The repeated use of "My son," suggests both the maturity of the writer and the immaturity of the youthful group to which he addressed his counsel. No advice is more needed by people in every generation.

The second portion of the book, 10:1 – 22:16, is properly called the Proverbs. The personal address, "My son," and other personal exhortations are missing. Each verse contains a proverb, consisting of two lines. Constant contrast is drawn between the righteous and the wicked, and between right and wrong. There is an abundance of practical application. By comparing Scripture with Scripture, the heavenly wisdom in these terse sayings is readily apparent.

In the third portion, 22:17 through chapter 24, there are basic instructions. The familiar address, "My son," is resumed in this section. The well-known exhortation, "My son, give me thine heart, and let thine eyes observe my ways," is addressed to a son and not a sinner, although often applied to the latter.

The fourth portion, chapters 25 — 29, contains the Proverbs of Solomon, collected by the men of Hezekiah. Who these men were is not known, but their accomplishments indicate that a revival of literary activity accompanied the revival of religion and national prosperity which marked the reign of Hezekiah. The agricultural emphasis suggests that the purpose of the instruction was economic rather than ethical. It magnified agricultural life at a time when the rural population was being attracted to the prosperity and profligacy of the cities, and was endangered by "pride, fullness of bread, and abundance of idleness."

The last section, chapters 30 and 31, contains the prayer and instruction of Agur to Ithiel and Ucal, and the oracles taught King Lemuel by his mother. Some have identified both Agur and Lemuel as Solomon, the latter probably being a pet name known to his mother. The closing portion is a description of a virtuous woman and is quite different from the rest of the book.

Many Proverbs were based on actual experiences. For instance, Proverbs 1:7 might have referred to the profligacy of Eli's sons; 1:10 could be an illustration by the experiences of Adam and Balaam; 4:14, that of Lot and David; and 12:11, possibly Abimilech and Absalom.

Ecclesiastes — Poems of Vanities

The historical background of Proverbs is the prosperous state of Israel in the time of Solomon. The setting of Ecclesiastes is the powerful and prosperous life of Solomon himself. To understand this book, one of the most difficult in the Bible, its contents must be regarded as a partial autobiography of the writer.

The keys to this book are two expressions, "vanity of vanities," which occurs thirty-four times, and "under the sun," found thirty-one times. One would expect the autobiography of a man as wealthy and wise and wondrous as Solomon to be highly optimistic. Instead, this man, who had all pleasures and honors, chariots, horses, palaces, and great possessions, found that all of them were "vanity and vexation of spirit." He represents the whole human race in asking the great question, "Is life worth living?"

After exhausting every experience that his power, wealth, and wisdom could provide, Solomon "hated life." The work that was wrought "under the sun" was grievous unto him, for "all was vanity and vexation of spirit." Like Solomon, anyone who lives merely in the light and beneficence of the sun is doomed to disappointment. Any man who looks beyond the great source of heat and light to its Creator and Controller will find Him, the only One who actually satisfies spiritual hunger.

Solomon failed because he thought that, with so many of this world's blessings, he did not need God. Deuteronomy contains special instructions for the future kings of Israel.[5] Solomon disregarded these admonitions. Life became a great personal disappointment to Solomon because he turned his back upon the Word of God and the God of the Word.[6]

Some have called this Solomon's "Penitential Discourse," probably composed shortly before his death. However, unlike Psalm 51, David's "Penitential Psalm," there is no confession of sin, and his reflection "vanity and vexation of spirit" is more expressive of disappointment than an acknowledgment of wrongdoing. Ecclesiastes is neither an admission nor a concealment of sin in the inspired author. It is an illustration of the insufficiency of all "treasure on earth" to induce men to "lay up their treasures in heaven" and set their "affections on things above," "where Christ sitteth on the right hand of God."

Every Christian needs to ponder the closing admonition to "hear the conclusion of the whole matter: Fear God, and keep His commandments," and, "Remember now thy Creator in the days of thy youth."[7]

Song of Solomon — Fidelity in Song

This book is also known as Canticles, or the Song of Songs, thus indicating that it was the most unique of the 1,005 songs composed by Solomon.[8]

The word "God" does not appear in Song of Solomon. This peculiarity and the fact that Song of Solomon is not quoted in the New Testament have led some to question its right to be included in the canon of inspired Scripture. In spite of this, it has always been a part of the Old Testament canon. Christ and His disciples recognized it as such, and the agreement of its material and language with other passages of Scripture sufficiently proves it inspired of God.

Two characters speak and act throughout—Shelomoh, a masculine name, and Shulamith, a feminine form of the same name. There is also a chorus of virgin daughters of Jerusalem. Toward the close, two brothers of Shulamith appear. As in most Hebrew poetry, there are no breaks to indicate a change of scene or of character. These must be determined partly by the sense, but chiefly by the use of the feminine and masculine pronouns in the original.

This love song was written at a time when polygamy was almost universal. Some Bible scholars say that it is a protest against polygamy and that is the story of a simple country girl, a Shulamite, from the vineyards of the north country, who is taken from her home and her espoused husband to be one of the numerous wives of King Solomon in Jerusalem. Although offered every inducement, she resists the efforts of Solomon to win her love away from the one to whom she had plighted her troth, whose praises she sings in her waking hours and of whom she dreams at night.

Dr. H. A. Ironside, in his book, *Addresses on the Song of Solomon*, suggests that the expression, "My own vineyard have I not kept," may well be the key to the interpretation of the book.

According to Dr. Ironside, the principle character of this song lived in the north country, in the mountain district of Ephraim. She belonged to an Ephraimite family which had charge of one of King Solomon's vineyards. Apparently her father was dead, but there was a mother, at least two brothers, and one sister, a mere child. This older daughter, the Shulamite, appears to have borne the brunt of the family responsibilities. Her brothers did not appreciate her and assigned difficult tasks to her. She worked hard and late for others, and had little time for herself, hence the confession, "They made me the keeper of the vineyards; but my own vineyard have I not kept." She had little opportunity to care for her own person, so she says, "Look not upon me, because I am black, because the sun hath looked upon me."

One day, while caring for her flock, she looked up and to her embarrassment, there stood a tall, handsome stranger-shepherd, who seemed to be drawn to her in sympathy because of her hard lot and uncomely appearance. Her modest confession to him went a long way toward a friendship which ripened into affection and into love. When he went away he said, "Some day I am coming for you, and I am going to make you my bride." She believed him, but probably no one else did. Her brothers did not believe him. The people in the mountain country felt that the poor, simple, country maiden had been deceived by this stranger. He was gone a long time. Sometimes she would dream of him and exclaim, "The voice of my beloved," only to find that all was quiet and dark about her; but still she trusted. One day he came back at the head of a glorious procession to claim her as his bride.

Dr. Ironside points out that this interpretation best fits the story of the Shepherd that can be traced from Genesis to Revelation and tells of Him who came down from heaven's highest glory into this dark world to win a bride for Himself. When He went away, He said, "I will come again, and receive you unto Myself." His Church has waited long for Him to come back, and some day He is coming to fulfill His Word.

In all ages both Jews and Christians have maintained that this book, which is more than a love song, has yielded a spiritual interpretation. They may have differed in the details of its application, but they agree that it foreshadows the relationship of Jehovah to Israel, or of Christ to His Church. Much misunderstanding of the book is the result of a poor translation and arrangement of the material of the text. This may be offset by the consistent use of accepted evangelical commentaries and by careful comparison of the various translations and versions of the Bible.

NOTES

1 Luke 4:23; cf. John 16:25, 29
2 Matthew 13:57; Mark 6:4; John 4:44
3 I Kings 4:32
4 Proverbs 9:10
5 Deuteronomy 17:16-20
6 Cf. I Kings 10:26 — 11:8
7 Ecclesiastes 12:1, 13
8 I Kings 4:32
9 John 14:6

FOR REVIEW AND DISCUSSION

1. List several practical truths in Proverbs which apply today.
2. Why was Solomon eminently fitted to answer the great question, "Is life worth living?"
3. How does Solomon's "Penitential Discourse" differ from David's "Penitential Psalm"?
4. Compare the philosophy of the world as seen in Ecclesiastes with your own philosophy.
5. Show how our love for Christ should compare with the love Solomon's bride had for him.

FOR ADDITIONAL ENRICHMENT

IRONSIDE, H. A. *Addresses on the Song of Solomon*. New York: Loizeaux Bros., 1933, reprint 1971.

————. *Notes on the Book of Proverbs*. New York: Loizeaux Bros., 1908, 7th ptg. 1971.

JENNINGS, F. C. *Old Groans and New Songs: Ecclesiastes*. New York: Loizeaux Bros., n.d.

LEUPOLD, H. C. *Exposition of Ecclesiastes*. Columbus: Wartburg Press, 1953.

UNDERSTANDING
THE PROPHETIC BOOKS

5

Prophecy is a term often used to designate all divine revelation since it was communicated by the Spirit of God to prophets first, and by them to men in general.[1] On Sinai's summit, God spoke directly to His chosen people, but this demonstration of His majesty was so dreadful that they entreated God to speak only through Moses.[2] After that, God revealed Himself through men who were directed to deliver His message to the people. Although most prophets lived in simplicity and poverty, and usually in some out-of-the-way place, these men of God had much authority among the people and were highly esteemed by godly rulers.

The law provided the death penalty against false prophets who assumed the role of a divinely sent messenger. False prophets were to be recognized either from their attempt to introduce idolatrous worship or by their predictions that failed to come to pass.[3] Despite the severity of this punishment, unauthorized messengers frequently appeared. No less than four hundred were present to contradict the divine counsel of Micaiah.[4] Jeremiah had to withstand the popular predictions of Hananiah and Shemaiah, who were recognized as patriots, while the prophet of God was decreed a traitor. However, God vindicated His prophets by fulfilling their predictions and dealt with the false prophets by bringing them to an inglorious end.[5]

PREPARATION OF THE PROPHETS

Most prophets received formalized training. Samuel was the first to institute a training school for prophets. It was located during his lifetime at Ramah.[6] Other schools were later established at Bethel,

Jericho, Gilgal, and elsewhere.[7] These schools gathered consecrated and promising students and trained them for their office. So successful were these institutions that, from the time of Samuel to Malachi, there never was a lack of official prophets. The enrollment in these schools differed from year to year. One elderly or leading prophet, called father or master, presided over them.[8] The chief curriculum was the Law and its interpretation.

Not all students who enrolled in these schools of the prophets possessed the prophetic gift, and not all inspired prophets were graduates of these institutions. Amos, although called to the prophetic *office,* did not belong to the prophetic *order* and had not been trained in the prophetical schools of that day.

PURPOSE OF THE PROPHETS

Oral teaching, as distinct from symbolic, was tacitly transferred from the priestly to the prophetic order. Why did the priesthood, which was ordained for this purpose under the Mosaic dispensation, surrender the teaching ministry? Since the prophetic order ceased to exist in New Testament times, evidently it was a temporary agency called into existence when the regular means of national instruction failed. Samuel established the school of the prophets shortly after the corruption of the priest's office by the sacrileges of Eli's sons.[9] When King Jehoshaphat revived the teaching ministry, it was necessary for him to enlist the priests for this purpose. This might indicate that the priests had failed to carry out the work to which they had been assigned. The ministry of the prophets was not a substitute, but a supplement for an appointed agency that had failed to function.

There is a clear distinction between the early and later prophets. The early prophets were forthtellers — the latter were foretellers. This does not infer that the predictive element in Scripture is limited to the prophetic books. Foretelling is found in nearly every book of the Bible, but it is not until the closing portions of the Old and New Testaments that the writings are devoted almost exclusively to this purpose. Nor did all the utterances of these latter prophets concern the future. The prophet was sent by God to deliver a divine message, which may or may not contain predictions. The later prophets were commanded to preserve their message in writing.[10] This fact is a strong argument for recognizing their reference to the future.

EMPHASES OF THE PROPHETS

Prophets may be grouped *geographically.* This does not mean that their ministry was solely for a particular field. Some of the prophets, like Isaiah, included both Hebrew and Gentile nations in their messages, but their primary concern seems to have been the people in particular areas, as shown in the following chart:

Israel	Judah		Gentiles
Hosea	Isaiah	Daniel	Jonah
Amos	Jeremiah	Haggai	Nahum
Micah	Joel	Zechariah	Habakkuk
	Zephaniah	Malachi	Obadiah
	Ezekiel		

The prophets may also be classified *chronologically* into four periods. The decline and collapse of the northern kingdom occurred during the Assyrian supremacy. After Israel was carried into captivity, the prophets centered attention upon Judah. In the meantime, the Assyrian kingdom was overshadowed by the Babylonian monarchy. This interval of time is generally recognized as the Chaldean period. When Judah was carried into Babylon, the exiled prophets still prophesied. After the restoration of the remnant to Jerusalem, a fourth period of prophecy began.

Assyrian	Chaldean	Exilic	Post-Exilic
Jonah	Jeremiah	Ezekiel	Haggai
Hosea	Nahum	Obadiah	Zechariah
Joel	Zephaniah	Daniel	Malachi
Amos	Habakkuk		
Micah			
Isaiah			

MESSAGE OF THE PROPHETS

The prophets did not record their prophecies until the ninth century before Christ. It became evident that the kingdoms of both Israel and Judah would go steadily downward, and these prophecies were necessary to remind the faithful remnant of a coming Messiah and a future period of restoration and blessing. The prophets spoke at times of matters pertaining to their own day. On other occasions they predicted events in the remote future. At least seven periods of time were included in their predictions:

Life period of the prophet
Time of Israel's captivity
Time of destruction of Israel's enemies

First restoration of Israel
First advent of Christ
Final restoration of Israel
Second advent of Christ
Some predictions had an early or partial fulfillment, awaiting the complete fulfillment in the more remote future. This is known as the *law of double reference*. Two passages in Isaiah illustrate this law. In chapter 44 Isaiah speaks of a restoration of Jerusalm. A study of Ezra and Nehemiah indicates that this was only partial and temporary at that time. In another passage, Isaiah 11:11, the prophet declares that "the Lord shall set His hand again the *second* time to recover the remnant of His people," and he is looking into the remote future to a complete and permanent restoration of Israel.

Observe that while the prophets spoke of the suffering Messiah, they also had a vision of the reigning Messiah. The prophets themselves were perplexed at this revelation of the duality of Christ's experiences, a mystery which was explained only after the crucifixion and resurrection of Christ.[11] It was not revealed to the prophets that there would be two advents of Christ with a long interval between. To them, His suffering and His reigning appeared to be contemporaneous. Time has revealed that Christ was first to redeem through suffering and later return to reign in glory.

Prophecy and History

The books of the prophets cover the same ground historically as the books of Kings and Chronicles, but the approach is entirely different. In the narrative of the Kings, the movement of the nation is observed with only an occasional glimpse of what God was doing and saying. In the prophetic record, on the other hand, God's utterances are given with only occasional reference to the narrative of the people. While some of the annals of Israel are duplicated, as in Isaiah 36 — 39, supplementary information is also given as in Jeremiah 40 — 44.

To understand and appreciate the prophets, the student must have a working knowledge of the historical background in the books of Kings and Chronicles. For example, the first verse of Isaiah gives the names of four kings who were reigning while Isaiah was prophesying. By referring to the accounts of these reigns in the books of Kings, the student becomes familiar with the evils which Isaiah had to combat.

Prophecy and Miracles

Prophecies and miracles are major and direct proofs of the supernatural character of the Bible. Nevertheless, they must be evaluated against the background of the general character of the whole scheme to which they belong. The Bible's miracles, its prophecies, its morals, its propagation, and its adaptation to human needs are the chief evidences of Christianity. None of these can be clearly understood if taken separately. Their unity provides the strongest evidence of all. Predictions were delivered to serve as evidence on which faith might reasonably rest, as stated specifically by our Lord: "And now I have told you before it come to pass, that, when it is come to pass, ye might believe."[12]

The evidence of prophecy is more convincing and enduring than that of miracles. A miracle may be performed chiefly for the immediate conviction of those who witnessed and experienced it. Prophecy, on the other hand, generally increases in value with the passing of the years. Time wears out and destroys almost everything else, but it emphasizes the value and significance of prophecy.

FULFILLED PROPHECY

Fullfilled prophecy is one of the best evidences that the Bible is the Word of God. No other book has ventured to reveal history in advance.

The highly improbable predictions of the prophets also constitute one of the best proofs of the verbal inspiration of their utterances. The prophets did not have full knowledge of all things about which they spoke and wrote. This is plainly stated. Daniel says, "And I heard, but I understood not."[13] Zechariah expresses his ignorance in a similar way.[14] After uttering their predictions, however, the prophets occupied themselves in searching into the full meaning of their words. Peter, writing of the prophets provides this instructive information:

"Of which salvation the prophets have inquired and searched diligently, who prophesied of the grace that should come unto you; searching what, or what manner of time the Spirit of Christ which was in them did signify, when it testified beforehand the sufferings of Christ, and the glory that should follow. Unto whom it was revealed, that not unto themselves, but unto us they did minister the things, which are now reported unto you by them that have preached the gospel unto you with the Holy Ghost sent down from heaven" (I Pet. 1:10-12).

The Holy Ghost through the prophets testified of the salvation that would be brought to men through the crucifixion and coronation of Jesus Christ.

NOTES

1 II Peter 1:20, 21
2 Deuteronomy 5:27, 28
3 Deuteronomy 13:1-11; 18:20-22
4 I Kings 22:6
5 Jeremiah 28:15-17; 29:30-32
6 I Samuel 19:19, 20
7 II Kings 2:3, 5; 4:38; 6:1
8 I Samuel 10:12; 19:20; II Kings 2:3
9 I Samuel 3:13
10 Jeremiah 36:2
11 I Peter 1:8-12
12 John 14:29
13 Daniel 12:8
14 Zechariah 4:5

FOR REVIEW AND DISCUSSION

1. How were false prophets recognized and punished?
2. Why did the prophets assume the teaching ministry?
3. Explain the law of double reference.
4. Explain the difference between the narrative in the Kings and Chronicles and the prophetic record of the kingdom period.
5. Compare prophecy and miracles as verifying God's Word.

FOR ADDITIONAL ENRICHMENT

ARCHER, GLEASON L., JR. A Survey of Old Testament Introduction. Chicago: Moody Press, 1964.

SCHULTZ, S. J. The Old Testament Speaks. New York: Harper & Row, 1960.

SCROGGIE, W. G. The Unfolding Drama of Redemption, Vol. I. London: Pickering & Inglis, Ltd., 1953.

THE GREAT MESSIANIC PROPHET

6

Isaiah

Isaiah was one of the greatest Hebrew prophets as well as a poet, a statesman, and an orator. He was bold, fearless, and sincere and did not hesitate to face a wicked king nor to proclaim the most unwelcome truth. He did not seek popular favor, but unsparingly denounced the sins of kings, priests, and all the people. Although stern and uncompromising, he showed tenderness of heart. He proclaimed comfort as well as judgment, and he clearly distinguished between God's love for the sinner and His hatred for sin.

Isaiah's ancestry is not fully known; but apparently he was born in Jerusalem and resided there during his significant public ministry. He prophesied during the reigns of Uzziah, Jotham, Ahaz, and Hezekiah, and was a contemporary of Hosea, Nahum, and Micah.

TIMES OF ISAIAH

Isaiah lived in times that called for men of great courage. The northern kingdom, saturated with idolatry, was rapidly approaching final destruction. Religious revivals under Hezekiah and Josiah, for which both Isaiah and Jeremiah were responsible, spared the southern kingdom for one hundred thirty years longer, thus delaying a similar fate for it.

Isaiah witnessed rapid commercial and military development of his nation. Under the long reign of Uzziah, Judah attained a degree of prosperity and power not enjoyed since Solomon. A large standing army and strong fortifications brought success in war. A port for commerce on the Red Sea and enlarged inland trade greatly increased the wealth of the nation. This prosperity brought inevitable avarice, oppression, and corruption in business and politics. Wealthy farmers used their power to exploit the common people. The worship of God was a mere formality and a hypocritical pretense.

MESSAGE OF ISAIAH

Isaiah stands preeminent among Old Testament writers in clarity of prophetic delineation regarding the person, character, and work of the Messiah. He is the "evangelical prophet" and his book is sometimes called the fifth gospel. His direct manner of presenting the sufferings and the kingdom of the Messiah has made his prophecies invaluable as established proofs that the Lord Jesus was He of whom the prophets spoke.

Not all of his writings have been preserved. It is distinctly stated that he composed the complete annals of Uzziah's reign, as well as the outstanding events of the more notable and worthy rule of Hezekiah.[1] This implies that he survived Judah's righteous king and fell into the hands of Manasseh, his cruel and wicked successor. Jewish tradition asserts that Isaiah suffered martyrdom by a terrible death. If Isaiah survived Hezekiah, he must have lived to be nearly ninety and exercised the office of prophet for at least sixty years.

The prophecies of Isaiah are eminently sublime and magnificent in their style and symbolic expression. They are more frequently quoted in the New Testament than any other Old Testament book except the Psalms. Quotations are made from forty-seven of the sixty-six chapters.

Symbolic actions, like those which frequently occur in Jeremiah and Ezekiel, are seldom found in Isaiah. The same is true of visions. The only one recorded is in chapter 6.

The book of Isaiah is a Bible in itself. It contains sixty-six chapters. The first thirty-nine have to do largely with the life and spirit of Old Testament judgments and warnings, while the last twenty-seven chapters anticipate the New Testament spirit of grace and restoration.

The main theme of the entire book is *God's deliverances*. The prophet first speaks of the deliverances from Syria and from Israel in the days of Ahaz, and the rescue from the more formidable power of Assyria, foreshadowed to Ahaz and more fully declared to Hezekiah. But the greatest deliverance of all was from Babylon.

PROPHECIES OF JUDGMENT (Chapters 1 — 35)

While still a youth, Isaiah had a marvelous vision. God's purity and holiness stood out in sharp contrast to the sham and self-righteousness all about him. Like John on Patmos, Isaiah was overwhelmed by a sense of his own sinfulness and that of the nation. His confession of sin was followed by his cleansing and consecration for the task to which God had called him. He knew in advance that there would be little response to his preaching or to that of all the other prophets whom God would send to reprove the people. The kingdom would grow weaker and weaker until its final overthrow. Only a few would be spared, but for the sake of that remnant, God would show mercy, and through them would bring in the blessings of the Messiah.

The first Messianic promise in chapter 2 was given when so much had been prophesied of impending catastrophe that the agelong promise of a redeemer was in danger of being forgotten. Hence the later and more specific prediction of the virgin birth in chapter 7. A later prophecy in chapter 9 pictures the bursting forth of a brilliant light in the midst of darkness, and enumerates the four great titles and the supernatural endowments of the One who is to sit on David's throne. What a marvelous contrast to the weak, vacillating ruler who then occupied the throne! Instead of the apostate conditions which prevailed under Ahaz, the ideal King will bless the world with righteousness and truth.

Judah and Israel (Chapters 1 — 12)

The first portion of Isaiah's predictions portrays the ungodly alliance of Judah with Assyria. When Isaiah began to prophesy, "in the year that King Uzziah died," the northern kingdom had already become a tributary of Assyria. Pekah, their ambitious, unscrupulous ruler, conceived the plan of throwing off the Assyrian bondage by first allying himself with Rezin, king of Damascus, then plundering Judah, and finally facing Assyria.

The first step having been taken, the second was attempted. Pekah and Rezin attacked Jerusalem with a combined army. In his fright, Ahaz, king of Judah, made an alliance with Assyria. Isaiah was sent to quiet his fears and warn him against foreign alliances. He advised Ahaz to put his trust in the Lord alone. He foretold that Assyria should destroy Syria and Israel, and punish Judah. Even in these severe judgments, the prophet spoke of God's mercy and predicted the future glory of God's people and the reign of the Messianic King.

Most of the early prophecies of Isaiah were soon fulfilled, thus confirming the faith of the people in the more remote predictions which characterize the latter portion of the book. Syria and Israel were to be subdued by Assyria before the infant son of the prophet could say, "My father," and Israel was to go into captivity in sixty-five years. As a sign to confirm this announcement, God revealed the virgin birth of Immanuel. To Ahaz this sign meant that within the brief period of a child's infancy, the enemies of Judah would be overthrown, but this celebrated passage also sets forth the birth of Christ.

Gentile Nations (Chapters 13 — 24)

The prophet then uttered a series of prophecies depicting the downfall of the nations to whom both Israel and Judah in their desperate condition had looked for assistance. These included Babylon, Philistia, Moab, Syria, Eygpt and Ethiopia, Edom and Arabia, and Tyre.

The questions may arise, "Why were these Gentile prophecies written and not spoken to the people addressed? Why were they preserved when these nations had long since ceased to exist?" These prophecies and their fullfillment were divinely recorded so that in these latter days men might have their faith confirmed, and that God's purpose to restore the Jews to Palestine and to bring them again in right relation to those people dwelling immediately around them might be revealed.

The prophecy concerning the fall of Babylon and its king contains unusually striking language. The date of this prophecy was definitely established at the time when Babylon was just entering its era of greatest magnificence. The announcement of Babylon's overthrow by the Medes was unbelievable, except for the fact that Isaiah's message was supernatural.[2]

Special interest has centered, for years, in the description of Lucifer in chapter 14. Some regard this as a description of the future Antichrist. Others associate it with Ezekiel 28 and believe that both passages reveal a glimpse of prehistoric days when Satan, the instigator of the king of Babylon, led the angels in a rebellion against God.

After pronouncing the impending woe that was in store for the countries surrounding Palestine, the prophet painted a picture of judgment which included all nations. The prophet concluded his denunciation of Israel's enemies by predicting the ultimate triumph and blessings of the people of God. The discourses against the nations are grouped together.[3] The promises for Judah are found at the end, like the finale of an oratorio.

Israel — Then and Future (Chapters 25 — 35)

Following the judgments of the Gentile world, Judah is seen as redeemed from her iniquity, delivered from her tribulations, and restored to her land.

Chapters 28 to 35 deal chiefly with Judah's futile alliance with Egypt. The fall of Samaria and the captivity of Israel took place six years after Ahaz' death.[4] Then Assyria, in fulfillment of prophecy, demanded tribute from Judah. King Hezekiah meekly complied, and even stripped the gold from the Temple doors to meet the assessment. At the same time he negotiated a protective alliance with Egypt, which Isaiah called a "covenant with death," a drunken nightmare, a shame, a useless fight against God, and a fatal blow to Jerusalem.[5] Egypt's aid was to no avail and is typical of the end of the age when Jerusalem, besieged by the Gentile nations, will vainly turn to the world for help. Isaiah again announced the Messiah as the only hope for a kingdom of stability and permanence, completely under divine control. Millennial blessings are portrayed; the faithful are seen dwelling in safety; and the King is reigning in His beauty.

HISTORICAL SECTION — HEZEKIAH'S REIGN (Chapters 36 — 39)

The historical section of Isaiah, located between the prophecies of judgment and those of consolation, is largely repeated in II Kings.[6] The purpose of this duplication was to remind God's people that when they repented of their sins and turned to Him with their whole heart, He would interpose for their protection and preservation. It also predicts that eventually Babylon and not Assyria would conquer Judah.

When the victorious Sennacherib overwhelmed Israel, there seemed to be nothing to prevent his taking Jerusalem. The blasphemous oration of Rabshakeh, the pleading prayer of Hezekiah, the promised deliverance by Isaiah, and the annihilation of the Assyrian host, followed in rapid succession. These prove God's divine intervention and faithfulness. Rabshakeh well admitted that the gods of the other nations were not able to deliver them out of the hands of Assyria. But he overreached himself when he challenged the God of Judah to prove His power to save His people. Hezekiah's confession of faith avowed that the gods of the fallen nations were idols and proclaimed that the God of Israel was greater than all the gods of Assyria.

No sooner had the Assyrians been banished forever from the land of Judah, than Hezekiah's sickness brought him in contact with the future conquerors of Jerusalem. Hezekiah made a fatal mistake in showing his treasures to the messengers from Babylon. The covetous visitors did not forget the wealth of Jerusalem or the rich embellishments of the Temple. True to Isaiah's prediction, the armies of Chaldea later returned and carried away to Babylon all these treasures and the most prominent families of the city.

PROPHECIES OF CONSOLATION (Chapters 40 — 66)

The characteristic note of the first part of the book of Isaiah is *judgment;* the dominate note of the second part is *comfort.* The prophet learned at the time he received his commission, chapter 6, that the people would not heed his call to repent, and that a succession of judgments would fall on them "until the cities be wasted without inhabitant, and the houses without man, and the land be utterly desolate." But paralleling his proclamations of judgment on the majority of the people, Isaiah spoke consolation and cheer, especially to the faithful remnant, concerning the promised Messianic King.

The second division of the book is a continuous prophetic discourse. It deals first with the deliverance from Babylonian captivity; second, the revelation of the Messiah; and third, the glory of the millennial kingdom.

Future Comfort for Israel (Chapters 40 — 48)

The opening section of the "New Testament" portion of Isaiah is one of the grandest descriptions of the greatness of God. Isaiah compared the gods of the seemingly invincible Babylon with the God of conquered and crushed Judah. But it is not His omnipotence so much as His omniscience that is demonstrated, for the prophet challenged the gods of Babylon to prove their divinity by predicting things to come.

Following this challenge, the prophet disclosed his credentials as a divine ambassador by revealing one of the most remarkable predictions in the Bible. God was going to deliver Judah from captivity and exile by the hand of a great Persian king who would be raised up "from the north" to conquer Babylon. The name of this great deliverer, Cyrus, was proclaimed one hundred and fifty years before he was born, and the prophet vividly saw the picture of his conquest as if the event were then transpiring. Cyrus was to be God's instrument for delivering Judah, as Nebuchadnezzar was the instrument in bringing upon them the predicted judgment.[7] The fall of Babylon would be the end of the exile, because Cyrus would restore their freedom and permit them to return to their own land. Isaiah assured them that they should fear no ill, for nothing could prevent their deliverance.

Of Cyrus, it is written, he shall be "the anointed," "my shepherd," the one "whose right hand the Lord upholdeth," "who performs all the Lord's pleasure." He is, in this sense, a type of a greater anointed one, the Redeemer of Israel, whose coming will mean a greater and a permanent restoration of Judah.

The Servant of Jehovah (Chapters 49 — 57)

The announcement of Cyrus as the deliverer of Judah paved the way for Isaiah to present the unparalleled picture of the future redeemer of both Jews and Gentiles. This was not Isaiah's first announcement of the Messiah. From the very beginning, his utterances include some Messianic revelation, and the majestic figure of the King looms up more and more clearly in subsequent chapters. In the second division of the book He occupies the center of the stage as the suffering Servant of Jehovah and the glorious King of Israel. Here the prophet reaches the climax of his Messianic utterances. The famous fifty-third chapter presents an almost complete picture of the sufferings of Christ seven hundred years before He appeared on earth. The greatest biblical expositors interpret this chapter as the story of the cross. It is repeatedly quoted in the New Testament as having its fulfillment in the Man of Sorrows. This was the chapter the eunuch of Ethiopia was reading and studying when Philip joined him and declared the description to be that of Christ.[8]

How the obedient Servant was to be treated by men is first mentioned in 50:6, but the culmination of His vicarious death is reached when He is "brought as a lamb to the slaughter." As a lamb He suffered in patience. He had done no violence, nor was deceit in His mouth. He suffered and died for others. It was the Father who smote Him, bruised Him, and put Him to grief. There is in the whole Bible no grander unfolding of John 3:16 — the gospel in a nutshell — than in Isaiah 53. But the prophecy does not end with the Messiah on the cross. It beholds His grave and sees Him risen, exalted, interceding, justifying many.

The Coming Kingdom (Chapters 58 — 66)

After this great vision, "Servant of the Lord" is not mentioned again nor His sufferings. His glorification comes more fully into view from here on until the end of the book. Perhaps the most striking passage is the one with which Christ announces His ministry:

"The Spirit of the Lord God is upon Me; because the Lord hath anointed Me to preach good tidings unto the meek; He hath sent Me to bind up the brokenhearted, to proclaim liberty to the captives, and the opening of the prison to them that are bound; to proclaim the acceptable year of the Lord." (Isa. 61:1, 2)

When Christ went into the synagogue at Nazareth and was asked to read from the book of Isaiah, He chose this passage, and then proclaimed: "This day is this Scripture fulfilled in your ears." He closed the book without finishing the prophecy because it was not to be fulfilled until He comes a second time — comes in power and glory.[9]

The day of vengeance is ushered in by the coming of the Avenger, Christ, on behalf of His people against the oppressing Gentiles. Then follows the intercessory prayer of penitent Israel in that day. This prayer should be compared with that of Nehemiah and of Daniel.[10] The answer to Israel's prayer is found in the concluding chapters. There Isaiah describes Israel's ultimate blessings in the millennium and the eternal state. The redeemed of all nations are pictured sharing Israel's blessings, while the unsaved are consigned to eternal punishment.

NOTES

[1] II Chronicles 26:22; 32:32
[2] Isaiah 13:17
[3] Isaiah 13 — 24
[4] II Kings 18:10
[5] Isaiah 28 — 32
[6] Cf. Isaiah 36 — 39; II Kings 18 — 20
[7] Jeremiah 25:9
[8] Acts 8:27-35
[9] Luke 4:20
[10] Nehemiah 1; Daniel 9

FOR REVIEW AND DISCUSSION

1. What basic principles in choosing a life work can be observed in Isaiah's preparation for the prophetical role in chapter 6?
2. State some Messianic prophecies in the first portion of the book of Isaiah.
3. What two words sum up the first and second parts of Isaiah?
4. Describe the Messiah as presented in the second division of Isaiah's prophecy.
5. Explain why Christ did not finish reading the passage from the prophet Isaiah in the synagogue at Nazareth (61:1, 2; cf. Luke 4:18, 19).

FOR ADDITIONAL ENRICHMENT

ARCHER, GLEASON L., JR. A Survey of Old Testament Introduction. Chicago: Moody Press, 1964.

JENNINGS, F. C. Studies in Isaiah. Rev. ed. New York: Loizeaux Bros., 1966.

MEYER, F. B. Christ in Isaiah. Ft. Washington, Pa.: Christian Literature Crusade, 1962.

SLEMMING C. W.The Bible Digest. Kregel Publications: Grand Rapids, 1968.

PROPHECIES OF JUDGMENT UPON JUDAH

7

Jeremiah and Lamentations

In the Septuagint Version, Jeremiah and Lamentations are one book. The common author is quickly discerned.

Jeremiah

Jeremiah's prophecies bear the prophet's name. No writer except Moses contributed more to the Old Testament. The book of Jeremiah constitutes approximately five percent of all Scripture and, with the exception of the Psalms, is the longest of the sixty-six books of the Bible. It is a rare combination of history, biography, and prophecy, recording not only the personal history of the prophet, but his messages of impending judgment, and the coming of the Branch of Righteousness and His glorious reign.

Unlike Isaiah, Jeremiah spoke frequently of his own experiences, in fact, more than any other Old Testament character. In this respect he may be compared with the Apostle Paul. Isaiah prophesied during a time of apostasy and lived to see some of his warnings heeded in the religious revival under Hezekiah, but Jeremiah's entreaties, uttered sixty-six years later, found little or no response.

Few men of God have had more bitter experiences than Jeremiah, the prophet of many sorrows. His kindred betrayed him, and the people of his native town threatened his life if he continued to utter unwelcome predictions. So completely was everyone arrayed against him, that he called himself "a man of contention to the whole earth." Because of the unsettled political conditions during which he prophesied, he was divinely commanded not to marry. He was also forbidden to enter the house of joy and feasting. Reproach and ridicule were his daily portion. Like Job, he cursed the day of his birth.[1]

Jeremiah's first predictions occurred during the righteous rule of Josiah. After the tragic death of this last godly king of Judah, Jeremiah mournfully prophesied the evil days of the successively wicked reigns of Jehoahaz, Jehoiakim, Jehoiachin, and Zedekiah, a period of more than forty years.[2]

JEREMIAH'S CALL AND COMMISSION (Chapter 1)

Before his birth, Jeremiah was called by the Lord, in the village of Anathoth, to be the prophet of Jerusalem's last days. While he was still young, he was assigned the arduous task of rooting out, pulling down, destroying, throwing down, building, and planting. He had to proclaim Jerusalem's downfall and the Babylonian captivity before he could declare the exiles' return and the city's rebuilding. He did speak about both, but the times called primarily for the clear teaching of the doom of Judah's capital, a message which cost him a lifetime of sorrow and suffering.

PROPHECIES DURING THE REIGN OF JOSIAH (Chapters 2 — 12)

The discourses in this section were probably delivered prior to the finding of the book of the Law in the temple.[3] This explains their moderate tone as compared with the later ones. Chapter 11 describes Jeremiah's persecution inflicted by the townspeople, which led him to take up a long ministry in Jerusalem, assisting in the reformation under Josiah.

PROPHECIES DURING THE REIGN OF JEHOIAKIM
First Series (Chapters 13 — 20)

In chapters 13, 18, 19, the prophet used symbols to dramatize his prophecies. The linen girdle typified Judah, whose pride would be marred when they "sat by the rivers of Babylon and wept." The wine bottles dashed one against the other symbolized Judah's sin-intoxication and destruction. The potter's clay represented Judah with whom God would do as He pleased. The broken earthen vessel illustrated how the people and the city would be broken. As a result of these proclamations, Jeremiah was cruelly beaten and put in stocks by Pashur, whose unhappy fate is then disclosed.

Second Series (Chapters 25, 26, 35, 36)

These chapters call attention to Jeremiah's constant exhortations. They announce that Judah and the surrounding nations would be brought into subjection by Nebuchadnezzar, who had just ascended the throne of Babylon. Jeremiah prophesied the success of the Chaldean army and urged submission to the Babylonians, declaring Nebuchadnezzar to be the servant of the Lord. For this he was proclaimed a traitor. And though his death was demanded, he was providentially protected.

The exact 70-year-period of the exile here predicted was later recalled by Daniel and led him to make his great intercessory prayer for the return of the captives.[4]

PROPHECIES DURING THE REIGN OF ZEDEKIAH

First Series (Chapters 21 — 24)

These chapters resulted from the king's inquiry regarding the outcome of Nebuchadnezzar's siege of Jerusalem. Chapter 22 sets forth the sad fate of Judah's last kings. The good king Josiah, who died in battle, was not to be mourned, but rather his son Shallum, Jehoahaz, who had been carried to Egypt.[5] They did not need to lament for unworthy Jehoiakim, who was dead. Coniah, Jeconiah or Jehoiachin, his son, was already a captive and would be a lifelong prisoner in Babylon. The house of David had been perpetuated from the time of Solomon, but no future heir of Coniah would sit upon the throne. How then can Christ, the son of David, assert His royal rights to the throne? The answer is simple. Jesus was able to fulfill these prophecies through Mary, His mother, who was a direct descendant of Nathan, the son of David.

Second Series (Chapters 27 — 34, 37 — 39)

Submission to the Babylonian yoke was urged in chapter 27, and the sad fate of the false prophet Hananiah, who predicted an early deliverance, was foretold. Jeremiah appeared on the streets of Jerusalem with a yoke on his neck to typify the Chaldean bondage. A false prophet destroyed Jeremiah's yoke, at the same time predicting that the Jewish exiles already in Babylon would return in two years.

The prophet foretold the Jew's wandering among the nations, and the final restoration of the Davidic kingdom with Christ sitting on the throne. Jeremiah purchased ancestral property at Anathoth as a visible expression of his faith in the fulfillment of this prophecy. The proclamation of Zedekiah's tragic fate and the destruction of Jerusalem were foretold by Jeremiah.

During the final siege of Jerusalem, the Egyptian army came to Judah's relief and the Chaldeans temporarily withdrew. This created a dangerous situation for Jeremiah who tried to escape from the city. He was arrested, accused of deserting to the Chaldeans and thrown into a dungeon. But he was saved from death by the intervention of Zedekiah the king.

When the city capitulated, Nebuchadnezzar protected Jeremiah and gave him the privilege of either accompanying the captives to Babylon, or remaining at Jerusalem with the governor, Gedaliah. Jeremiah chose to remain and mourn over the sad fate of the fallen city and to comfort the melancholy remnant.

PROPHECIES DURING THE EXILE (Chapters 40 — 44)

The assassination of Gedaliah threw the colony into confusion and many, fearing the wrath of Nebuchadnezzar, urged flight into Egypt. Jeremiah, however, assured them of safety in Judah and destruction in Egypt. Again they spurned his counsel and forced him to emigrate with the others to Egypt. Until his death, Jeremiah continued to prophesy against Egypt and the surrounding nations, including Babylon, the conqueror of them all. His last message, probably delivered after the remnant was settled in Egypt, concluded with the ringing challenge: "All the remnant of Judah, that have gone into the land of Egypt to sojourn there, shall know whose words shall stand, mine, or theirs."[6]

PROPHECIES CONCERNING GENTILE NATIONS (Chapters 45 — 52)

These chapters include a collection of prophecies that were uttered at different times during Jeremiah's ministry. While chapter 45 is a message to Jeremiah's servant, Baruch, the remaining chapters relate to Egypt, Philistia, Moab, Ammon, Edom, Damascus, Hazor, Elam, and Babylon. The predictions against Babylon minutely describe, in one of the long chapters in the Bible, the final siege and downfall of that great world power. Will Babylon be rebuilt? Was this overthrow by Cyrus a shadow of great destruction in the future? A comparison of Jeremiah 51:63, 64 with Revelation 18:21 is helpful in understanding Jeremiah's message.

Jeremiah prophesied of what is commonly known as "the times of the Gentiles," during which Israel would be scattered among the nations without a king and without a temple. Naturally kings, princes, priests, and people were opposed to such a prophecy, and there were many false prophets willing to predict what was pleasing to the people. These false prophets were accepted as patriots, while Jeremiah was called a traitor, all of which conspired to make his life the most unhappy of all the prophets. When the false prophets proclaimed peace, he announced war. When they foretold prosperity, he declared captivity. He was always unpopular, since his message to Judah predicted her rejection of God and the transfer of earthly dominion into the hands of the Gentiles. Although Jeremiah had a reputation for tears, his tears were not for himself; they were for others. Despite this display of emotions, the prophet was a man of great courage, declaring the whole counsel of God, unpopular and unwelcome as it was. Never did he flinch under persecutions. When priests and prophets and common people conspired to kill him, he shed "a world of tears" for his dying nation. In this respect, he was a type of Christ. As Jeremiah wept over the body of Josiah, so Christ wept at the grave of Lazarus. As the prophet wept over Jerusalem, he typified that greater Prophet who shed tears as He approached the city for the last time.[7] Like Christ, Jeremiah was not "without honor save in his own country." He, too, was "a man of sorrows and acquainted with grief."

Lamentations

These lamentations reveal the weeping prophet. They are composed after the manner of funeral hymns, and are an eye witness account of the ruins of the city and of the Temple. Jeremiah's prediction of the ruinous work of Nebuchadnezzar had been fulfilled. These lamentations are a mourner's utterances, "every letter written with a tear, and every word, the sound of a broken heart."

The book consists of five chapters, each a separate and complete poem. Each song contains twenty-two verses, according to the number of letters in the Hebrew alphabet. In the third song, each verse is divided into three sentences, making sixty-six verses in our English translation. The entire book is an acrostic — a favorite form of Hebrew poetry.

NOTES

[1] Jeremiah 11:21; 15:10; 16:2; 16:8; 20:8; 20:14
[2] II Chronicles 35:25; Jeremiah 1:2, 3
[3] II Kings 22:3-13
[4] Daniel 9:2
[5] II Kings 23:34
[6] Jeremiah 44:28
[7] Luke 19:41

FOR REVIEW AND DISCUSSION

1. What prediction did Jeremiah make concerning the duration of the Jews' exile in Babylon?
2. Why was Jeremiah so unpopular?
3. Why was Jeremiah called the weeping prophet?
4. What great principles of faith can be observed in the life of Jeremiah?
5. What was the occasion for Jeremiah writing the book of Lamentations?

FOR ADDITIONAL ENRICHMENT

IRONSIDE, H. A. *Notes on the Prophecy and Lamentations of Jeremiah.* New York: Loizeaux Bros., 1950.

LAETSCH, THEO. *Jeremiah: Bible Commentary.* St. Louis: Concordia Pub. House, 1952.

MORGAN, G. CAMPELL. *Studies in the Prophecy of Jeremiah.* Westwood, N.J.: Fleming H. Revell Co., 1955.

PROPHECY OF RESTORATION   8

Ezekiel

Two of the four outstanding Old Testament prophets were priests — Jeremiah and Ezekiel. Their ministries were contemporary. Jeremiah had an active part in the stirring events which took place during the downfall of Jerusalem. Ezekiel viewed these happenings from afar and wrote largely of the relation of these events to the exiles of which he was a member. Ezekiel revealed little of himself, and his ministry of twenty-two years was only half that of Jeremiah's.

Another contemporary of Ezekiel was Daniel who also prophesied from outside Jerusalem. While Daniel served as the political prophet of the exile, Ezekiel wrote as a priest. These two books present a clear illustration of the political and religious parallels which run through the Old Testament.

Nebuchadnezzar captured Jerusalem twice — in 605 B.C. and in 597 B.C. On the first occasion he learned of his father's death and, in his haste to return to Babylon, was satisfied to take back only the Temple vessels and a few captives, including Daniel. At that time, the city was spared from further plunder. Nine years later, when Jehoiakim rebelled, Nebuchadnezzar again appeared before Jerusalem, and Jehoiakim was bound in chains to be carried to Babylon.[1]

His son, Jehoiachin, who also was called Coniah, was enthroned as the vassal of Nebuchadnezzar. Three months later, on showing symptoms of disaffection, Jehoiachin was likewise deposed and led away captive. This time the Chaldeans thoroughly plundered the city, carrying away all the treasures and ten thousand of the nobles and artisans, leaving only "the poorest sort of the people of the land." Ezekiel was taken with this latter group of exiles.[2]

EZEKIEL THE PROPHET

Nebuchadnezzar established the captives as a Jewish colony at Tel-abib, on the banks of the river Chebar. Ezekiel lived in his own house and ministered as pastor, prophet, and priest to his unhappy people. As pastor, he performed his responsibilities as vigilant watchman. As prophet, he proclaimed impending judgment and future restoration. As priest, he possessed a keen and accurate knowledge of all forms of worship.

After five years at Tel-abib, Ezekiel exercised his prophetic ministry. Jeremiah who had already prophesied thirty-four years, sent a special letter to the Jewish colony in exile.[3] This was the occasion of Ezekiel's first utterance. It appears that false prophets had deluded the captives into anticipating an early return to Jerusalem. To dispel this false hope, Jeremiah sent his message, "For thus saith the Lord, That after seventy years be accomplished at Babylon I will visit you, and perform my good word toward you, in causing you to return to this place."[4] Ezekiel's ministry confirmed Jeremiah's unwelcome predictions during the five years that were to elapse before Jerusalem's final overthrow in 586 B.C. After that catastrophe, his great restoration messages comforted the disappointed and heartbroken people.

Compared with Jeremiah

While both Jeremiah and Ezekiel contributed messages of warning and exhortation, they were widely different in temperament. Jeremiah prophesied of a dying nation, and his tender, loving sympathies are everywhere apparent. Ezekiel lacked these emotional characteristics. He had great energy and vigor, and his stern, deep sense of responsibility made his condemnations far more severe than those of Jeremiah. When he launched his attack against the crimes and prevarications of an apostate people, he did it with vehemence and warmth of feeling.

Ezekiel's style of writing was different from that of Jeremiah. His visions concerning the future were greater and far more complete. He used his God-given title "son of man" at least one hundred times in his writing. Only one other prophet, Daniel, is thus designated in the Old Testament. Christ applied this same appellation to Himself eighty-six times. As characterizing one who was rejected, it appropriately applies to both.

Use of Symbolism

Ezekiel illustrated his predictions with dramatically striking symbolism. He lay on his side and ate polluted bread by weight and drank water by measure to show the hardships of the siege. For another prophecy, he shaved off his hair and beard, and then burnt a third of it, cut a third with a knife, and cast the remaining third to the winds to typify the triple fate that awaited the doomed citizens of Jerusalem.

Ezekiel also employed symbolic visions, often difficult to understand. The parable of the fire in the south forest is an illustration.[5] Only Daniel and Revelation have more elaborate symbolism. Whatever the interpretation of these prophecies, the prophet reiterated his commission to be a *"sign* unto the house of Israel." The captives were deeply prejudiced against Ezekiel's messages and sometimes turned deaf ears to his unwelcome words.

Concern for the Temple

Being a priest, Ezekiel was concerned about the Temple. He had painfully witnessed its plundering by Nebuchadnezzar. In the first portion of his writings, he mentioned God's throne in the Temple. Later, he spoke of its removal from Jerusalem because the government of earth was taken from Israel and conferred upon the Gentiles. At the close, however, he saw God's throne restored in the millennial Temple.

EZEKIEL'S PROPHECIES

The contents of Ezekiel fall into three divisions. The first twenty-four chapters contain prophecies of judgment on Judah. The second division presents prophecies of judgment upon the Gentile nations, and the third, prophecies of restoration.

Prophecies of Judgment on Judah (Chapters 1 — 24)

The prophecies of the first division were delivered before the destruction of Jerusalem. They are grouped according to the year in which they were given, and Ezekiel is exact in specifying the time of his utterances. Ezekiel's call to the prophetic ministry was not until the fifth year of King Jehoiachin's captivity, and his predictions of the period may be divided into prophecies during the fifth, sixth, seventh, and ninth years of captivity.

During the Fifth Year of Captivity (Chapters 1 — 7)

The opening chapters explain the prophet's call and commission. Seven times he was warned that he was being sent to a *rebellious* nation. He was solemnly instructed to "warn the wicked from his wicked way." Next followed the symbolical representations of the imminent siege and destruction of Jerusalem. The 390 years of Israel's apostasy and the 40 years in which Judah had been especially rebellious were set forth in a typical siege. Ezekiel directed all these prophecies to "the whole house of Israel" rather than to Israel or Judah individually, as the pre-exilic prophets had done. This was probably because Judah was now too near its end to be saved by further warning. The "time of the Gentiles" had already begun, so the prophet looked forward to the day when Israel would share with Judah a permanent restoration.

During the Sixth Year of Captivity (Chapters 8 — 19)

This section opens with particular references to Judah and Jerusalem. In the presence of the elders of Judah, Ezekiel presents his vision of the profaning of the Temple, and describes the resultant judgment on Jerusalem and the priests, a few faithful being marked for exception. The symbol of the divine presence is consequently withdrawn, first from the Temple and then from the city.

The prophet was carried back in captivity to "the rebellious house." He warned by the sign of digging through the wall that Zedekiah in this manner would vainly endeavor to escape from his Chaldean captors. He reproved the false prophets who were busy in Jerusalem and Babylon proclaiming peace and early restoration. When interviewed by the elders of Israel, he reiterated his warning of impending destruction, saying that even if Noah, Daniel, and Job were in Jerusalem to intercede, the city could not be spared.

He set forth Israel as a fruitless vine, and as a base adulteress. Using an eagle to symbolize Nebuchadnezzar, he showed how the top of the cedar, Jehoiachin, had already been plucked and carried away, and that the vine which was left, Zedekiah, would turn to the other great eagle, Pharaoh. The prophet vindicated God's justice and showed the equity of His moral government. Chapter 19 is a lamentation over the sad fate of the kings, Jehoahaz, Jehoiachin, and Zedekiah.

During the Seventh Year of Captivity (Chapters 20 — 23)

The elders of Judah came to ask Ezekiel about the outcome of Zedekiah's revolt against Babylon and alliance with Egypt. He reminded them of Israel's idolatry in Egypt, and reproved their own deep-seated idolatry. He predicted that Zedekiah would be overthrown and that both the priesthood and the royalty would disappear until He whose right it is to rule should return. The next two chapters expose the immoral conditions in Jerusalem and vindicate God's justice in the judgment and destruction of the city.

During the Ninth Year of Captivity (Chapter 24)

Two and one-half years elasped before the prophet's next utterance. At the beginning of Jerusalem's last siege, Ezekiel was advised not only of this fact, but of the sudden death of his wife, for whom he was commanded not to mourn. His indifferent attitude was to be a sign of the people's hardened hearts in the midst of impending disaster. From that hour, the prophet was not to open his mouth on the subject of Jerusalem until he should receive the news of its capitulation.

Prophecies of Judgment Upon the Gentile Nations (Chapters 25 — 32, 35)

During the siege of Jerusalem, Ezekiel wrote the future history of the seven contemporary nations which surrounded Judah. Passing briefly over Ammon, Moab, Edom, and Philistia, which were already decadent nations, he wrote more at length of Tyre and Egypt.

The prophecies concerning Tyre are of special interest. With marvelous detail, the Chaldean siege of fourteen years was described. While the city was eventually taken, Nebuchadnezzar was unable to take the island fortress, and the method that Alexander the Great used 240 years later to accomplish this was minutely told. The prophet referred to the king of Tyre, and to his instigator, Satan, and gave a glimpse of Satan's prehistoric glory, pride, and humiliation. Special attention was given to the fate of Egypt and its rulers, since Judah's rebellion against Babylon had been inspired by fond hopes of assistance from this powerful ally. Egypt's golden sun was setting, and henceforth it could not exalt itself above the nations nor rule over them. [6]

Prophecies of Restoration (Chapters 33, 34, 36 — 48)

The third division of the book is introduced by a warning to Ezekiel of his responsibility as a watchman. A special messenger told of Jerusalem's downfall. This was the signal for Ezekiel to resume prophecies concerning his own people. His subsequent utterances were largely devoted to the future restoration of both Israel and Judah. In the vision of the valley of dry bones, there is a clear prediction concerning the united northern and southern kingdoms, with David (Christ) once more King over the united kingdom. This cannot refer entirely to the partial restoration under Ezra and Nehemiah as that pertained to only a portion of Judah. Chapters 38 and 39 reveal Israel's last enemies, Gog and Magog, and their destruction. The concluding chapters describe the millennial Temple. This subject was of special interest to the priestly writer of the restoration. All the prophets predicted the ultimate return of the remnant and the glory of the Messianic kingdom. Ezekiel alone described the detail of the new order to be established. He alone disclosed the pattern of the new Temple, its new ritual, and the new division of the land.

NOTES

[1] II Chronicles 36:6, 7
[2] II Kings 24:12-16; Ezekiel 1:1, 2
[3] Jeremiah 29
[4] Jeremiah 29:10
[5] Ezekiel 20:45-49
[6] Ezekiel 29:15; II Kings 24:7

FOR REVIEW AND DISCUSSION

1. When, where, and with whom did Ezekiel go into captivity?
2. Compare the prophet Ezekiel with Jeremiah.
3. What title which Christ used was Ezekiel often given?
4. How did Ezekiel's occupation as a priest affect his writings?
5. Briefly summarize Ezekiel's prophecies of restoration.

FOR ADDITIONAL ENRICHMENT

ARCHER, GLEASON L., JR. *A Survey of Old Testament Introduction.* Chicago: Moody Press, 1964.

BLACKWOOD, ANDREW W. *Ezekiel, Prophecy of Hope.* Grand Rapids: Baker Book House, 1965.

ELLISON, H. L. *Ezekiel: The Man and His Message.* Grand Rapids: Wm. B. Eerdmans Publishing Co., 1958.

SCHULTZ, SAMUEL J. *The Old Testament Speaks.* New York: Harper & Row, 1960.

GREAT PROPHECIES OF WORLD EMPIRES

9

Daniel

Daniel, meaning *God is my judge*, was a prince of the royal house of David. In 605 B.C., as a youth, he was carried captive into Babylon along with some other princes of Judah by Nebuchadnezzar. Jeremiah had already been prophesying for twenty-three years. This was nine years before Ezekiel went into exile and twelve years before he began to prophesy. Daniel lived throughout the whole period of the captivity and was nearly ninety years old when Zerubbabel led the first expedition back to Jerusalem. He exercised his prophetic office longer than either of his contemporaries, Jeremiah or Ezekiel, the seventy years of his ministry far exceeding that of any other Old Testament seer.

Daniel was of princely descent and personal charm. He was chosen with three other promising young Hebrews, Shadrach, Meshach, and Abednego, to be trained for the king's service. Through his abstinence, diligence, brilliance, and his reliance upon God, he gained favor and advancement. He had early been impressed with the truth, perhaps at his mother's knee, that "the king's heart is in the hand of the Lord, as the rivers of water; He turneth it whithersoever He will."[1] He knew that to please God was to please the king. Not that Nebuchadnezzar cared about Daniel's pleasing God, but because God, being pleased with Daniel, would incline the heart of the king favorably toward him. Daniel served as prime minister under four dynasties of the world's greatest powers.

Daniel is mentioned by Ezekiel, not as a writer, but as a righteous and wise man.[2] Ezekiel's recognition of Daniel's righteousness is seen by his mention of Daniel with Noah and Job. Daniel's wisdom is compared with that of the king of Tyre. Ezekiel declared, "There is no secret that they can hide from thee," suggesting Daniel's famous interpretation of Nebuchadnezzar's dream was well known to Ezekiel. Although Daniel's name is not mentioned in the great faith chapter of Hebrews, his deeds are recorded.[3]

Daniel's deep piety, humility, and dependence upon God are alluded to in nearly every chapter of his book. He was a great man of prayer. His intercession for the forgiveness and restoration of Israel in chapter 9 is one of the most wonderful prayers recorded in the Bible. He talked with angels, and the angel Gabriel addressed him three times as the "man greatly beloved." In this respect, he was like the Apostle John. Both Daniel and John were greatly loved of God, and they were granted a larger outlook on the future than any other prophet. Their visions of the glorified Christ were also similar.[4]

The book of Daniel was written in two languages. Chapter 1 — 2:4 and chapters 8 through 12 were written in Hebrew. The portion from 2:4 through chapter 7 was in Aramaic, the language of those eastern empires. The purpose for this is clear. Daniel recorded in the Chaldean tongue what pertained to world history. He used the Hebrew for what concerned his own people.

HISTORICAL SECTION (Chapters 1 — 6)

The first six chapters of the book of Daniel are mainly historical. Except for the recorded experiences of Shadrach, Meshach, and Abednego in the fiery furnace, all have to do with Daniel and his relationship with the monarchs of the great kingdoms of Babylon and Medo-Persia.

Nebuchadnezzar (Chapters 2 — 4)

The second chapter is prophetic as well as historic in that the interpretation of Nebuchadnezzar's dream referred to future events. The king dreamed of an image of a man who represented four successive world empires. The head of gold was Nebuchadnezzar, an absolute autocrat. The arms and breast of silver represented Medo-Persia, a limited monarchy. The thighs of brass represented Greece, which was weaker than the preceding governments because it was divided into four parts after Alexander's death. The legs and feet of iron represented Rome, which lasted longer, but was weaker than the others because it was divided into the eastern and western empires, represented by the two legs. The feet of clay mingled with iron forecast the development of democracy in later times. The development of these four great world empires has been confirmed in history. What is more significant, conquerors like Mohammed, Charlemagne, and Napoleon have never been able to establish a fifth universal kingdom. The world waits "the kingdom that shall never be destroyed" and "the Stone cut out of the mountain without hands," which shall dash the rebellious nations "in pieces like a potter's vessel."[5] Thus we see that the Messiah and His kingdom are major subjects of prophecy.

The fourth chapter also contains prophecy, for Daniel's interpretation of Nebuchadnezzar's second dream was fulfilled a year later. The proud monarch, boasting of his accomplishments and his right to honor and homage, became suddenly insane and incapacitated for a period of seven years. Isaiah had previously described the vain ambition of the king of Babylon;[6] this no doubt was a prophecy of Nebuchadnezzar. History confirms both of these prophecies, for Nebuchadnezzar was humbled. But he was restored to praise and extol and honor the King of heaven.

Daniel's interpretation of Nebuchadnezzar's dream brought him to public attention and he was advanced to prime minister, making him first in both political and educational authority. Later, during the king's insanity, Daniel was presumably viceroy. In the meantime, Shadrach, Meshach, and Abednego were given high positions in the province of Babylon.

Belshazzar (Chapter 5)

Under Belshazzar, Daniel lost his prominent position. Later, at Belshazzar's feast, when the handwriting on the wall could not be deciphered by the wise men, the queen remembered Daniel's interpretation of Nebuchadnezzar's dreams. Upon her recommendation, Daniel was summoned to appear. The prophet rebuked the king for his impiety and pride, reminding him how Nebuchadnezzar had been humbled and deposed from his throne because "his heart was lifted up." He revealed how Belshazzar would be slain that night because of his idolatry, the city taken, and the Medo-Persian kingdom established.

Daniel's prediction regarding the fall of Babylon was fulfilled the same night he interpreted the handwriting on the wall. This confirmed the previous prophecies of Isaiah 13, Jeremiah 50 and 51, and

Habakkuk 2. Belshazzar was the grandson of Nebuchadnezzar and was reigning in Babylon while his father, Nabonidus, was warring with Cyrus. History speaks of Nabonidus and not Belshazzar as the son of Nebuchadnezzar. This is explained by the fact that the same Hebrew word is used to denote father and grandfather. Jeremiah 27:7 makes this quite clear: "All nations shall serve him (Nebuchadnezzar), and his son (Nabonidus), and his son's son (Belshazzar), until the very time of his land come."

Darius and Cyrus (Chapter 6)

Under Darius the Mede (538 B.C.), the kingdom was ruled by 120 princes over which there were three presidents, of whom Daniel was first. The king's preference for Daniel excited jealousy, and a plot was arranged to secure his downfall. This failed when God sent His angel and shut the lions' mouths. Daniel was advanced in years when cast into the lions' den, but he was as faithful to God in his old age as in his youth. His enemies hated him because of his determined opposition to bribery and corruption and because of his belief in the Word of God.

Under Cyrus the Persian (536 B.C.), the eighty-year-old Daniel continued in his high office. No doubt he was one of the king's counselors responsible for sending the Jews and their sacred treasure back to Jerusalem.

PROPHETIC SECTION (Chapters 7 — 12)

The last six chapters of Daniel constitute the prophetic portion. The four visions of the future history of the nations show the relationship to the Jewish people, including definite descriptions of the time and conditions associated with the coming of Christ.

Daniel's Visions (Chapters 7, 8)

The visions of chapters 7 and 8 occurred during the prophet's political retirement in the earlier years of Belshazzar. They cover the same area as Nebuchadnezzar's dream in the second chapter, but with more detail. In the seventh chapter, Babylon is represented by a lion, Medo-Persia by a bear, Greece by a leopard, and Rome by a nameless beast of frightful description. In the eighth chapter, Medo-Persia appears as a ram and Greece as a he-goat, whose "notable horn" was Alexander the Great. Daniel's vision of the "*one* like the Son of man" and the "Ancient of days" refers to the Messiah receiving His earthly kingdom from God Himself.[7] The "king of fierce countenance" is generally recognized as Antiochus Epiphanes, but the interpretation of 8:17-26 goes beyond Antiochus and speaks of the Antichrist in the last days.[8]

Seventy Weeks (Chapter 9)

The ninth chapter records Daniel's great prayer of intercession for his people. The fact that he "understood by books" proves that the previous prophecies had been recorded in writing. Apparently Daniel was a careful student of the Law and the Prophets. At least he was familiar with the predictions of Isaiah, of Jeremiah, and with Solomon's dedicatory prayer.[9] The faith of the aged prophet was rewarded by the restoration decree of Cyrus and by a revelation of Israel's future from the Babylonian exile to the end of the present age.[10]

The seventy weeks recorded in the last verses of chapter 9 was the exact time in which the interests of the Jewish people were to be in the ascendency. These weeks are sevens of years and are divided into three periods. First, the seven weeks, or forty-nine years, which saw the restoration of Jerusalem, recorded in the books of Ezra and Nehemiah; second, the sixty-two weeks, or 434 years unto the time of "Messiah the Prince"; and third, the one week, or seven years, the period of tribulation just preceding the Second Coming of Christ, when Israel shall again be in her own land.

Israel's Future (Chapters 10 — 12)

Chapter 10 is the key to the last three chapters, Daniel's preparation for his last prophecy. It is summed up, "I am come to make thee understand what shall befall thy people in the latter days."[11] The Bible's primary concern is with the nations that affect Palestine and the Jewish people. The first part of this final prophecy deals with the kings who were to rule the restored remnant in Jerusalem. The reference to the powerful reigns of Xerxes and Alexander centers attention upon the division of the Grecian empire among Alexander's four generals. Because Palestine lay between Egypt on the south and Syria on the north, the wars of these nations are described in detail. Antiochus Epiphanes is given detailed consideration. In fact, chapter 11 may be outlined as the dominion, deeds, and doom of Antiochus. The latter portion of the chapter describes his extenuated shadow, the Antichrist of the last days.

Chapter 12 predicts the last days, or the seventieth week, of Israel's predicted history. Daniel characterizes it simply, "a time of trouble, such as never was since there was a nation even to that same time." Then he is commanded to "shut up the words, and seal the book, even to the time of the end."

The Lord spoke distinctly of Daniel the prophet. In His great prophetical discourse in Matthew 24, He quoted Daniel and to understand that reference, it is necessary to understand Daniel. The book of Revelation, the major prophetic book in the New Testament, would be a sealed composition without the enlightenment of the book of Daniel. The unfulfilled prophecies in Daniel would likewise remain a mystery if their fullfillment were not recorded in Revelation.

Daniel as a statesman and prophet was vitally concerned about the welfare of his own people. In the panoramic view of the rise and fall of nations, Daniel was assured that his people Israel will ultimately triumph.

The Church Age, from the Jewish rejection of Christ to the beginning of Israel's seventieth week, is not in view in the book of Daniel. In the end time many will read Daniel's message with increased understanding. Although Daniel is informed about the resurrection of the just and unjust, he is not informed about the sequence nor given details beyond the fact that this will occur in the end time.

There is a close resemblance in the elevation from slave to sovereign in the lives of both Joseph and Daniel. This is a striking illustration of God's absolute control in the affairs of men and nations, and of the way He uses His children, even though captive, to direct the administration of kingdoms.

NOTES

[1] Proverbs 21:1
[2] Ezekiel 14:14, 20; 28:3
[3] Hebrews 11:33
[4] Cf. Daniel 10:5-10; Revelation 1:12-18
[5] Psalm 2:9
[6] Isaiah 14
[7] Daniel 7:9-14; cf. 2:34, 35; Luke 19:12, 15, 27; Zechariah 14:3-9; Revelation 19:11-16
[8] Cf. II Thessalonians 2:3, 4; Revelation 13
[9] Isaiah 44:28 — 45:3; Jeremiah 25:11, 12; I Kings 8:46-50
[10] Ezra 1:1-4
[11] Daniel 10:14

FOR REVIEW AND DISCUSSION

1. How were the ministries of Daniel, Ezekiel, and Jeremiah related?
2. Show how God blessed and used Daniel as a result of his purpose to be true to God.
3. What lessons can we learn for today's living from the lives of Daniel and his companions?
4. What chapter suggests that Daniel was a diligent student of the Scriptures?
5. How does the book of Daniel relate to the book of Revelation?

FOR ADDITIONAL ENRICHMENT

BOUTFLOWER, CHAS. *In and Around the Book of Daniel.* Grand Rapids: Zondervan Publishing House, 1963.

CULVER, R. D. *Daniel and the Latter Days.* Chicago: Moody Press, 1954.

McCLAIN, A. J. *Daniel's Prophecy of the Seventy Weeks.* Grand Rapids: Zondervan Publishing House, 1940.

WILSON, R. D. *Studies in the Book of Daniel (second series).* New York: Fleming H. Revell Co., 1938.

HOSEA, JOEL, AMOS, OBADIAH

10

The prophetic word demonstrates God's power and wisdom, and His response to man's need. Man is ignorant of what a day may bring forth, but God reveals His will and discloses His plans and purposes for the future. The prophetic portions constitute about one-fourth of Scripture content and demand careful and prayerful study.

Prophecy is not only a prediction of the future arising out of present conditions; it is inseparably related to God's will for men. It calls for complete and immediate obedience now.

The Minor Prophets are no less important or less inspired than the Major Prophets, but are so named because of their comparative brevity. In the Hebrew canon they appear as one book. Together they contain only one chapter more than Isaiah, and their 1,050 verses are far short of Jeremiah's 1,346 verses.

Hosea — The Prophecy of Divine Love

Hosea's prophetic ministry to Israel spanning about four decades, began during the reign of wicked Jeroboam II, and it is probable that his life and ministry ended at the destruction of the northern kingdom. He addressed his prophecies exclusively to the northern kingdom. Though a contemporary of Isaiah, he began his work some years earlier. Since his ministry covered a period of about forty years, the question may be raised as to why his writings are so brief. As is true with other prophets, it is probable that many of his utterances were never recorded. The Holy Spirit has preserved only such portions as He deemed profitable for our reproof, correction, and instruction in righteousness. Other Bible writers quote from Hosea either directly or indirectly over 30 times.

Hosea prophesied during the period when the northern kingdom was oppressed by the Assyrians. These circumstances and the ultimate extinction of Israel by Assyria are the burden of his prophecies. Assyria was to Israel what Babylon was to Judah — the appointed destroyer. Most of the prophets wrote about Judah. Only two or three of the minor prophets and earlier utterances of Isaiah concern Assyria.

The oppression by Assyria was the result of Israel's sin. Such a degree of idolatry, anarchy, tyranny, murder, adultery, drunkenness, lying, stealing, and other gross sins, had never before been practiced in Israel. The knowledge of God was forgotten. The priests were leaders in shame. New kings made their way to the throne after murdering their predecessors. Under such circumstances Hosea repeated God's warning, "I will cause the kingdom of the house of Israel to cease."

Hosea was a weeping prophet to Israel, as Jeremiah was to Judah. His tender entreaties seemed to flow in tears which almost blotted out the threatenings and accusations. The prophet passionately entreated Israel to return to God, assuring them of His forgiveness and favor, but Ephraim was joined to his idols, and divine judgment eventually fell with crushing force.

THE PROPHET'S LESSON (Chapters 1 — 3)

Hosea's tenderness characterized him as the prophet of love. His forgiving spirit toward his unfaithful wife was a fitting illustration of God's love for wayward Israel. The first three chapters of Hosea contain the personal narrative of Hosea's unhappy marital relationship. Gomer was Hosea's "prodigal wife." Again and again under the stress of temptation she sold herself to do evil. At last she deserted her husband and three children. She sank lower and lower. She was flung aside as a thing of shame and finally offered for sale in the slave market. Even then the prophet loved her, redeemed her from bondage, and gave her a place in his house again, where she sat desolate for many days.

The first three chapters are like an abridgment of the entire book. They set forth God's relationship to His people and reveal His tender love despite their rebellion and infidelity. Through the sorrow of

Hosea's own unrequited love, he understood God's grief over the spiritual adultery of His people. He knew the infinite love that made God willing to follow after Israel in order to win the people back to love and faithfulness.

THE PROPHET'S MESSAGE (Chapters 4 — 14)

Shifting from the illustration of the first three chapters, Hosea begins in chapter 4 to present the charges of God against Israel. He states, "There is no truth, nor mercy, nor knowledge of God in the land." The prophet also speaks of the willful ignorance of Israel, their idolatry, with the result that God would withdraw His face from Israel. Filtered through this indictment against Israel is Hosea's continual call for repentance on the part of His people.

Hosea's more remarkable predictions include the downfall of Samaria; the deliverance of Judah following Hezekiah's intercession; the punishment of Judah; and the final restoration of both Israel and Judah. This last passage is most significant. The regathering of Israel in the land of Palestine may well be a significant development in preparation for the time when they shall again "seek the Lord their God and David their king."

Joel — The Prophecy of Pentecost

The date of Joel has been much discussed. He makes no reference to Nineveh or Bablyon but does mention the Phoenicians, Philistines, Edomites, and Egyptians. His prophecy must have been written just before or after the period when the Assyrian and Chaldean world empires were supreme. The former view provides the least difficulties. This would make Joel the earliest prophet of Judah, his ministry beginning shortly after the days of Elijah and Elisha. Thus there would be a sequence of prophetic testimony from the dark days of the kingdom under the notorious Ahab to the end of Judah's existence.

REPENTANCE REQUIRED (Chapters 1:1 — 2:17)

More than half of Joel's prophecy is a description of the devastation by a plague of locusts. In all literature there are few descriptions comparable to this. In solemn tones the prophet speaks of this national calamity, calling for public mourning and humiliation.

Special attention is called to the destruction of the vines and the fruit trees. Afterward there is an inference that all plant life was consumed, "A fire devoureth before them; and behind them a flame burneth; the land is as the garden of Eden before them, and behind them a desolate wilderness; yea, and nothing shall escape them." So dense were the clouds of devastating insects that the sun was obscured and its light reduced as during an eclipse. The plague was accompanied by drought, for "the beasts of the field cry also unto Thee; for the rivers of waters are dried up."[1]

Joel used the scrouge of insects and the visitation of drought to foreshadow a greater ruin that would occur many years later. The locust plague, expressed as "palmerworm," "locust," "cankerworm," and "caterpillar," may have prefigured the four world powers of Babylon, Persia, Greece, and Rome, which successively devastated Judah. Perhaps the prophet foretold the events predicted in the book of Revelation, where locusts are used as a symbol of a destroying army.[2]

BLESSING PROMISED (Chapters 2:18 — 3:21)

The prophecy in the third chapter is of peculiar interest. The assembling of the nations in the valley of Jehoshaphat undoubtedly refers to the time when the nations are judged for their treatment of God's covenant people.[3] Instead of the nations beating their swords into plowshares,[4] the prophet sees a time of universal warfare preceding the millennium of peace. Hence, he cries, "Prepare war, wake up the mighty men, let all the men of war draw near; let them come up; beat your plowshares into swords, and your pruning hooks into spears."[5]

Other prophets refer to this great judgment of the Gentile nations.[6] In Revelation 16 and 19 it is spoken of as the Battle of Armageddon. Joel also sees the celestial perturbations and the disarrangement of the solar system ending the great tribulation period and ushering in the Second Coming of Christ.

But Joel speaks of blessings as well as judgments. He pictures temporal prosperity when the drought is broken by refreshing rains and the land once again becomes productive. He announces the special outpouring of the Holy Spirit, later used as the text of Peter's wonderful sermon on the Day of Pentecost recorded in Acts 2.

Finally, Joel describes the millennial blessing when "the Lord also shall roar out of Zion . . . the hope of His people, and the strength of the children of Israel." The importance and extent of Joel's prophecies are suggested in 1:3, "Tell ye your children of it, and let your children tell their children, and their children another generation."

Amos — The Pastoral Prophecies

Amos prophesied to Israel nearly two centuries after Solomon and one century after Elijah. He was an older contemporary of Hosea, but a generation ahead of Isaiah.

THE PROPHET AND HIS MESSAGE

Amos was a shepherd and a fruit farmer. He came from Tekoa, a small village six miles south of Bethlehem. Although a native of Judah, his mission was to the northern kingdom. He had not been trained in the prophetical schools. The Lord called him out from his flock and commanded, "Go, prophesy unto my people Israel."

The style of Amos was clear, direct, and powerful. His diction was sharp but not always elegant. His language fit the nature of his message. He drew his figures from the life he knew best. He shocked the cultured society of Bethel by comparing them with frightened cows. He expressed truth as he saw it. His language was pastoral. His imagination keen and practical. In his language and allusions he showed familiarity with the book of Deuteronomy.[7]

His prophecy is definitely dated as two years before the earthquake which happened in the days of Uzziah, king of Judah, during the reign of Jeroboam II.[8] In less than forty years, the northern kingdom was to fall, but just before the crash, there was the highest prosperity of her history. She was at peace with Syria. Assyria had not yet become a formidable power. Jeroboam II recovered much of the ancient kingdom of David and Solomon. His conquests included Damascus, Transjordan, Ammon, Moab, and even parts of Judah.[9]

The prosperity that grew out of such national prestige was ruinous. The rich built summer houses and winter palaces of ivory in which they lolled on silken cushions. They exploited the poor. Idolatry and corruption were terrible. The nation seemed to forget that idolatry has always resulted in shame and misery from the time Jeroboam I instituted calf worship at Bethel.[10]

Amos directed his prophecy against Bethel. This was not the political capital, but it appears to have been the largest and strongest city of the north. Here the priests and prophets made their homes and practiced the costly but hollow worship of "baptized paganism."

Amos opened his prophecy with an utterance from Joel 3:16 and closed his address with another quotation from Joel's prophecy. This suggests his acquaintance with the prophet who preceded him. His theme was national accountability for national sins. His drastic exhortation, "Prepare to meet thy God, O Israel," was directed to the nation that had so often pledged fidelity to Jehovah.

NATIONS CONDEMNED (Chapters 1, 2)

This farmer-prophet from a rival nation appeared in the midst of a corrupt court. This prejudiced his hearers. With remarkable tact, however, Amos aroused their interest and gained attention by first denouncing the enemies of Israel. He began with Syria, the hated neighbor of Israel. He proclaimed judgment on Israel's ancestral foes — Philistia and Tyre. Then the prophet came closer home by denouncing Edom, Ammon, and Moab, the blood relatives of Israel. His listeners must have been amazed when the rustic seer directed his fiery speech against his own people, Judah, which was perhaps the most hated of all Israel's foes. Then, as a climax, he concentrated his attack on Israel itself, "For three transgressions of Israel, and for four, I will not turn away the punishment thereof."

ISRAEL DENOUNCED (Chapters 3:1 — 9:10)

This backwoodsman dug beneath the veneer of temporal prosperity and exposed the inherent weakness and national decay that invited doom. Having addressed himself to the affairs of state, Amos assailed their apostate religion, of which Bethel was the center. Righteousness was his dominant note, necessary for the security of a nation and for the stability of religion. Where righteousness was lacking, no amount of ritual would ever avert impending judgment.

Knowing that his call to righteousness would be unheeded, the prophet quickly flashed a pronouncement of judgment. He alluded to the coming captivity of Israel. He visualized by five illustrations the doom of the nation. The first of these was the locust plague; the second, fire sweeping the nation. Both of these were averted by the prayer of the prophet. Then followed the vision of the plumb line, God's test of the nation's edifice so crudely and weakly constructed that it could not stand. The vision of the basket of summer fruits disclosed the rottenness of the nation that had repudiated the Word of God and proclaimed a famine, not of bread or water, "but of hearing the words of the Lord." In the last vision, he revealed the hopelessness of any escape from the vengeance of God, "Though they dig into hell, thence shall my hand take them; and though they climb up to heaven, thence will I bring them down."

These visions should have stirred his hearers even more than the direct denunciation of their sins. In the midst of his utterances, Amos was interrupted by Amaziah, priest of Bethel, who commanded him to hasten back to his own country and prophesy there. Amos modestly declared: "I was no prophet, neither was I a prophet's son; but I was an herdsman, and a gatherer of sycamore fruit; And the Lord took me as I followed the flock, and . . . said unto me, Go, prophesy unto My people Israel."[11]

RESTORATION PROMISED (Chapter 9:11 — Chapter 15)

Like all true prophets, Amos did not leave his hearers in the depths of despair. He revealed the brightness of a new day. In the last words of his address, he declared that God would release His people from captivity and "plant them upon their own land, and they shall no more be pulled up."[12] The signs in Palestine today suggest an early and complete fulfillment of these last words of the book.

Obadiah — Doom of Edom

Obadiah is the shortest Old Testament book. It was written exclusively for Edom, a foreign nation spoken of more frequently in prophetic Scripture than any other except Babylon. There are more than twenty different predictions recorded concerning Edom.[13]

Obadiah was written after Jerusalem was abandoned, its Temple destroyed, and every means of restoration removed. From their fortified dwelling place in rocky passes, the Edomites joyously viewed these misfortunes befalling their neighbors, but they had no apprehension for their own safety.

The Edomites were not immediately affected by the Chaldean operations in Syria, Palestine, and Egypt. By timely submission, they won the temporary favor of Nebuchadnezzar. In his invasion of Judah, they are named among his willing auxiliaries. They are represented as triumphing, with fiendish malignity, over the ruin of their kinsmen of whose desolate land they hoped to obtain a large portion for themselves.

This spiteful spirit demonstrated the ancient rivalry that existed between Esau and Jacob and their children — the two hostile nations of Edom and Israel. The Edomites hated Israel because God had prospered that nation in marked contrast to Edom. When Israel was journeying to the promised inheritance, Edom had refused passage through its borders.[14] From that time on, they pursued a vindictive policy against Israel. Their behavior toward God's chosen people marked the Edomites for divine judgments, in spite of their alliances and natural mountainous security.

Obadiah warned Edom that retribution was coming. Malachi's prophecy, one hundred fifty years later, shows that Edom had been driven out from his mountain, but had returned and built the desolate places, only to be completely overthrown later.[15] Ezekiel, who wrote at the same time as Obadiah, also accused Edom of perpetual hatred.[16] For this reason they are spoken of as "the people against whom the Lord hath indignation forever."[17]

No ruins are more imposing than those of Edom. Within a small area there are thirty ruined towns, absolutely deserted. The city of Petra, hewn out of the solid rock, is the relic of a metropolis of immense strength and one of the wonders of the world. "The pride of thine heart hath deceived thee, thou that dwellest in the clefts of the rock, whose habitation is high; that saith in his heart, Who shall bring me down to the ground?" For ages after these words were penned, Edom was prosperous and populous. It continued so even during the time of Christ. King Herod, who made an effort to destroy the newborn King of the Jews, was an Edomite, and his brutal slaughter of the innocent babes was characteristic of the race he represented. In A.D. 636, the Mohammedans overran the country, and the nation finally fell into the appalling desolation which had been predicted.

Obadiah, like Nahum and Habakkuk, concluded his prophecy by speaking of the future restoration of Israel. He carefully pointed out that then Israel shall possess the land of Esau.

NOTES

[1] Joel 1:18-20
[2] Revelation 9:7-10
[3] Cf. Matthew 25:31-46
[4] Micah 4:3; Isaiah 2:4
[5] Joel 3:9, 10
[6] Isaiah 34: 1-10; 63:1-4; Ezekiel 38:1 — 39:29; Zechariah 14:1-7

[7] Amos 2:10; 4:6-10, 11; 5:11; Deuteronomy 29:5; 28:22, 27, 60; 29:23; 28:30
[8] Zechariah 14:5
[9] II Kings 14:28; 13:5; Amos 1:13; 2:1-3
[10] I Kings 12:27-33
[11] Amos 7:14, 15
[12] Amos 9:11-15; cf. Acts 15:15-17
[13] Aside from Obadiah, the principal ones are Isaiah 34, 63; Jeremiah 49; Ezekiel 35
[14] Numbers 20:14-21
[15] Malachi 1:3-5
[16] Ezekiel 35:5
[17] Malachi 1:4

FOR REVIEW AND DISCUSSION

1. What is the reason for the distinction between the titles — Major Prophets and Minor Prophets?
2. What domestic tragedy helped Hosea understand God's love to Israel despite their infidelity?
3. Explain the future significance of the plague of locusts in Joel.
4. What remarkable tact did Amos use to gain a hearing?
5. What knowledge of the Edomites is necessary to understand Obadiah?

FOR ADDITIONAL ENRICHMENT

Gaebelein, A. C. *The Servant and the Dove: Obadiah and Jonah.* New York: Our Hope Press, 1946.

Ironside, H. A. *The Minor Prophets.* New York: Loizeaux Bros., Inc., 1909.

Laetsch, Theo. *Bible Commentary on the Minor Prophets.* St. Louis: Concordia Pub. House, 1956.

Morgan, G. Campell. *The Minor Prophets: The Men and Their Messages.* Westwood, N.J.: Fleming H. Revell Co., 1960.

Slemming, C. W. *The Bible Digest* (The Minor Prophets). Grand Rapids: Kregel Publications, 1968.

JONAH, MICAH, NAHUM, HABAKKUK

11

Except for Micah, who addressed his messages to both Israel and Judah, each of these minor prophets focused his attention on a foreign people: Jonah and Nahum on Nineveh, Habakkuk on Chaldea. These three minor prophets hardly referred to any nations other than those to whom they prophesied. Concerning their own nation, Israel, they offered only a bit of encouragement or rebuke, and that by way of contrast or comparison.

Jonah — Mercy to the Gentiles

When God commanded Elisha to anoint Hazael to be king of Syria, Elisha wept knowing that Hazael was divinely commissioned to afflict Israel and to take away much of their territory.[1] A large portion of this land, however, was regained during the powerful and prosperous reign of Jeroboam II. This was previously announced by Jonah,[2] probably during the reign of the predecessor of Jeroboam II, Joash, with whom Elisha had close contact and during whose reign he died.[3] Thus it will be seen Jonah might have been the earliest of the writing prophets, since he closely followed Elisha, the most eminent of the forthtellers.

While Jonah was a forthteller to Israel, his written message concerns Nineveh. Despite Israel's enlargement and prosperity under Jeroboam II, Assyria's conquest and growth made her an antagonist to be feared. Nineveh, the capital of the empire, was one of the oldest, largest, and strongest cities of that day. It was founded by Nimrod,[4] was ninety miles in circumference, and its population was approximately 600,000. It was a "garden city," with enclosed gardens and pastures that provided food for both man and beast. Its walls, built by Sennacherib, were some 40 to 50 feet high and they extended for two and one-half miles along the Tigris River and eight miles around the inner city.

Jonah was the only prophet who tried to conceal his message. He disclosed the reason for this in Jonah 4:2. The preservation of Nineveh meant the eventual conquest and destruction of Israel. Love of country and hatred of idolatry made his mission distasteful to him. He had no sympathy with God's plan to save a Gentile nation, so God had to deal with him miraculously in order to compel his obedience. The picture of the protesting, pouting prophet reluctantly reviewing the repentant heathen city is in sharp contrast to that of our gracious Lord weeping over His enemies in Jerusalem.

The great result of Jonah's prophecy was the repentance of this pagan city. This was an object lesson to Israel. Despite Israel's knowledge of the only true God; despite His many favors, blessings, deliverances, and interpositions in their behalf, the nation was steeped in idolatry. The prophets warned of judgment, but wayward Israel had turned a deaf ear. God then sent a forthteller to a pagan nation which would repent of its wickedness at one proclamation of judgment.

As Israel had rejected God's prophets, they later rejected His only begotten Son. In alluding to this, Christ declared that "the men of Nineveh shall rise up in judgment with this generation, and condemn it; because they repented at the preaching of Jonas; and, behold, a greater than Jonas is here."[5]

Christ's reference to Jonah is one of the strongest evidences of the truth of the narrative. The fact that He used the period of Jonah's burial in the great fish as a sign of the number of days He would spend in the grave proves the historicity of Jonah's experiences.[6] It is inconceivable that Jesus would have used a "myth" as a type of His own burial and resurrection. Both the disciples and the Jews accepted the experience of Jonah as fact. There is no more conclusive evidence in the Gospels. Even so, they were loathe to believe in the resurrection of Christ.

Jonah was a type of our Lord in His burial and resurrection. He also prefigured the history of the Jewish people. The great fish represents the Gentile nations who have swallowed up God's chosen people without assimilating them or destroying their identity. Hosea had the days of Israel's entombment in mind when he wrote, "After two days will He revive us; in the third day He will raise us up, and we shall live in His sight."[7]

Micah — The Prophecy of Universal Peace

Micah is the only minor prophet who addressed his messages to both Israel and Judah. His discourse is brief, yet it contains one of the most important Old Testament prophecies — a comprehensive description of the Messiah, His nature, kingdom, and work.[8]

Micah was called a Morasthite because he was a native of Moresh-gath in Philistia, about twenty miles west of Jerusalem. His full name was Micaiah. In many ways he resembled the forthteller by that name who predicted the tragic end of King Ahab.[9] Jeremiah referred to Micah as a bold and faithful witness, and declared that Judah listened to his voice and repented.[10]

Micah prophesied a few years after Amos and Hosea, during the reigns of Jotham, Ahaz, and Hezekiah, but before the fall of Samaria (722 B.C.). He was a contemporary of Isaiah. Isaiah was a man of the city, brought up in Jerusalem, probably in a home of wealth and refinement. Micah was born in a lowly village and probably died as he had lived, a poor man.

Isaiah was gifted with a wide outlook and a broad sympathy, so that he could interpret world politics. Micah, on the other hand, confined his gaze largely to Judah and Israel. Isaiah addressed the nation as a whole, especially the people of the city. Micah saw the wrongs of his own class, the common folk. He was the great prophet of social reform.

In his opening prophecy, Micah mentioned at least ten towns and villages near his home and warned them of approaching calamities. The meaning of the names of these towns heightened the effect of his poetry. Gath means *weeptown;* Aphrah, *dusthouse;* Saphir, *beauty-town.* These verses might be translated, "Weeptown, weep not; Dusthouse, roll thyself in the dust; Beautytown, go into captivity with thy beauty shamed." He lingered for a time near his birthplace, but Samaria and Jerusalem formed the chief subjects of his utterances. He foretold the invasion of Shalmaneser, Sennacherib, the dispersion of Israel, the cessation of prophecy, the utter destruction of Jerusalem, and some events in the more distant future.

JUDGMENT FOR SIN (Chapters 1 — 3)

The first chapter is Micah's arraignment of the house of Israel for its sins and for its contamination of Judah and Jerusalem. The second and third chapters are a bill of particulars in support of his general indictment. The prophet's greatest denunciation was the sin of oppression and he found the idle rich the most guilty. Prosperity, growing out of the long years of peace under Uzziah, had created a new class of wealthy men. Infatuated with their sudden fortune, they had become greedy for still more gain. These rich exploiters could not have oppressed the poor had they not been protected in their crime by the rulers whom God had appointed to safeguard the rights of the poor.

The prophet likened such exploitation of the poor to a cannibal feast. Then Micah pointed out the false prophet behind the idle rich and the corrupt politicians. Living on the bounty of the idle rich and basking in the favor of a depraved government, the false prophets justified the wicked for a reward, winked at their vices, and shared in their corruption.

PROPHECY OF SALVATION (Chapters 4, 5)

After proclaiming judgment on both Israel and Judah and arraigning these evildoers, the prophet told of a brighter and better day. He described the golden age of perpetual peace in which all nations of the earth will participate, when every man shall sit under his own vine and fig tree without fear of oppression or loss of property. These verses are frequently quoted today in support of universal peace, without recognition of the fact that the "He" referred to is the Prince of Peace, who must be enthroned at Jerusalem before that millennium of peace can be a reality.

Micah's great Messianic prophecy predicts the birthplace of our Lord. Though uttered seven hundred years prior to the Messiah's birth, it is one of the four major prophecies relative to this event. The Shiloh prophecy of Genesis 49:10 designates the *tribe* of Judah. Nathan's prophecy in II Samuel 7:26 reveals the *house* of David. The vision of the seventy weeks in Daniel 9:25 announces the *time*. Micah 5:2 discloses the *place*, Bethlehem. This prophecy was the answer given to Herod when he inquired where Christ was to be born.[11]

COVENANT CONTROVERSY (Chapters 6, 7)

The last portion of Micah sets forth the Lord's controversy with His people. Isaiah and Amos presented God in controversy with His people because of their sins. Micah presented Him in controversy with them because of their heartless, formal worship, which in God's sight is sin.

God reviewed His gracious dealings with Israel in the past. His appeal should have touched their hearts. What greater demonstration of love and longsuffering could be made? He had redeemed them from bondage, defended them from their enemies, supplied every need. In return God asked affection and companionship for Himself, and not costly and inhuman sacrifices. The climax of this controversy is 6:8, which some commentators regard as the greatest verse in the Old Testament: "He hath shewed thee, O man, what is good; and what doth the Lord require of thee, but to do justly, and to love mercy, and to walk humbly with thy God?"

The closing chapter is peculiarly striking — a soliloquy of repentance on Israel's part. Some of the people, at least, confessed and lamented their sinful condition and expressed confidence in God's returning favor. There are few verses in the Bible more expressive of quiet hope and trust than these promised blessings which were contingent upon Israel's return to the land and their request for forgiveness.

Micah has a remarkable prophecy respecting the capitals of Israel and Judah. Both Samaria and Jerusalem were flourishing at the time of the prophecy. That they should suffer the inglorious fate predicted for them seemed impossible. Of the capital of the northern kingdom, the prophet declared that the Lord would "make Samaria as a heap of a field, and as plantings of a vineyard," and "pour down the stones thereof into the valley," and "discover the foundations thereof."

Today, only the foundations of the ancient capital remain and the stones that have not been gathered in heaps have been "poured down into the valley." Of Jerusalem, the prophet said that Mount Zion would "be ploughed as a field." Like many ancient cities, Jerusalem has been besieged again and again. The Chaldeans "brake down the walls of Jerusalem round about,"[12] and when the Roman armies made the city a desolation, most of the ramparts were thrown down. The present walls were built by Sultan Suleiman, and Mount Zion, the city of David, was left outside the area he enclosed.

Nahum — Doom of Assyria

The prophecies concerning Gentile nations revealed two facts with astonishing accuracy and reality — the covenant people were to be chastened, but the nations used of God for this purpose were to be destroyed.

The book of Nahum is a continuation of Jonah. Both books are connected parts of the same moral history. Jonah records the repentance of Nineveh; Nahum predicts its destruction. The catastrophe is so tremendous that the fate of no other nation claims the prophet's attention.

At the time of Nahum's prophecy, Nineveh had been well known for several centuries. As early as the eighth century, it was a leading city of the Assyrian kingdom. Although immediate destruction was averted after Jonah's warning, Nahum now presents a forceful message of impending doom.

The word "Nahum" means *consolation*. This prophecy concerning the fall of Nineveh was cheering news to the inhabitants of Jerusalem. Assyria had been the hated enemy and oppressor of Israel and Judah for nearly two centuries. Their kings were cruel. Their captives were gruesomely mutilated. They were more aggressive, more idolatrous, more wicked, more feared than any other nation in ancient history. At the time of Nahum's prophecy, Assyria was at the zenith of international power.

DOOM OF NINEVEH (Chapter 1)

In his opening chapter Nahum portrays the majesty of God who is the sovereign and omnipotent ruler in nature. The wicked are only allowed to continue because God is slow to anger, but in due time the vengeance of a jealous God will be released. Assyria had imposed troubles on Jerusalem in the days of Hezekiah, but Nahum boldly assures his people that they need not fear affliction from Nineveh again. The coming judgment will be final.

For Judah, the doom of Nineveh signifies relief from oppression. The good news of freedom from fear constitutes an admonition to renew their religious devotion.

ASSAULT UPON NINEVEH (Chapter 2)

In the second chapter the prophet describes the siege, capture, spoliation, and annihilation of the great Assyrian capital. He pictured the scarlet uniforms and red shields of the Chaldean army marching to the attack while Saracus, king of Nineveh, vainly marshaled his troops for defense. "The gates of the rivers shall be opened, and the palace shall be dissolved."[13] History states that after the flood broke down the river gates, Saracus knew that the city was lost. He retreated to his palace and after setting it on fire, perished in the flames. Many valuables have been found in the ruins of the city, but no gold or silver. The Chaldeans completely fulfilled the prophecy, "Take ye of the spoil of silver, take the spoil of gold."[14]

The last part of the chapter speaks of the utter extinction of Nineveh. That so great and ancient a city should utterly disappear as to make its site uncertain creates interest among Bible scholars today.

RUIN OF NINEVEH (Chapter 3)

Nahum's predictions of impending doom seemed so impossible that he reminded the people of the disaster of No, which had recently been destroyed by Ashurbanipal. Nineveh also was strongly fortified. Its colossal walls were wide enough at the summit for chariots to be driven six abreast.

The Assyrian empire's collapse was sudden and surprising. It was brought about by the combined revolt of the Medes and Babylonians against the tyrant who then occupied the Assyrian throne. The siege of Nineveh lasted for two years, but the inhabitants saw no immediate cause of alarm for its safety. Then, an extraordinary overflow of the Tigris River carried away a large section of the impregnable walls behind which the Assyrians were confident and secure. The allied army entered by the breach and completed the ruin of the city.

History records all of these facts, and they are prophetically and dramatically portrayed by Nahum as he writes under the inspiration of the Holy Spirit.

Two outstanding truths in the prophecy of Nahum are revealed. First, God's faithfulness to His people. Second, however great His patience with His enemies, a day is coming when His wrath will be much more terrible because of that patience.

Habakkuk — Doom of Chaldea

Nineveh fell about 612 B.C. Probably after Nahum's prophecy had been fulfilled, Habakkuk revealed his vision of the overthrow of the Babylonian kingdom. The Assyrians were gone and the Chaldean kingdom was rising to triumph. The Chaldeans, not the Assyrians, were eventually to conquer Judah, and the prophecy of Habakkuk came when the tottering southern kingdom had recognized the imminent danger of the new world conqueror. Nebuchadnezzar already in 605 B.C. had taken Daniel and many nobles from Jerusalem into captivity, and that deportation was to be followed by a second, in 597 B.C. The final destruction of the city was in 586 B.C. Habakkuk's description seems to allude to all three.

Habakkuk, like Job, spoke about affliction. He wrote with pathos that resembled that of his contemporary, Jeremiah. Prophetically he saw the Chaldeans invade his native land, the Temple and the sacred worship abolished, the land devastated, and the people exiled. His prophecy is filled with scorn, derision, and desolation, but it is not without hope. His book contains all the glories and excellencies of poetic prophecy. It opens with one animated portraiture — the march of a conqueror, and closes with another — a sublime song of praise and prayer.

HABAKKUK'S COMPLAINTS (Chapters 1, 2)

The prophet writes in the form of a dialogue between himself and God. He first complained that the pagan Chaldeans were permitted to afflict God's children. God's answer shows His purpose to use Chaldea to discipline Judah for their shameful idolatry and oppression. Habakkuk's complaint about the permanence of evil is answered in the utter destruction of the Chaldean power. Chaldea was an instrument in God's hands, but she could not escape His judgment upon her own sins. These sins are enumerated: lust of empire; lust of wealth; lust of magnificence; lust of vice; and attachment to idolatry. The declaration and punishment of Nebuchadnezzar's pride, by his being deprived of his reason, was also predicted.[15] Habakkuk's prophecies were fulfilled about seventy years later in the fall of Babylon.

The book of Habakkuk contains several familiar passages. "The just shall live by faith" in 2:4 is referred to by Paul in Romans 1:17; Galatians 3:11; and Hebrews 10:38. The great prophecy that "the earth shall be filled with the knowledge of the glory of the Lord, as the waters cover the sea" is here repeated for the fifth time.[16] The last verse in chapter 2 is frequently used for public worship today: "The Lord is in His holy temple; let all the earth keep silence before Him."

HABAKKUK'S PRAYER OF PRAISE (Chapter 3)

Many hymns and prayers have reiterated Habakkuk's petition in 3:2, "O Lord, revive Thy work." Despite devastation, desolation, and dire distress, the book concludes with the sublime climax, "I will rejoice in the Lord, I will joy in the God of my salvation."

NOTES

[1] II Kings 8:12; 10:32; 13:22
[2] II Kings 14:25
[3] II Kings 13:14
[4] Genesis 10:11
[5] Matthew 12:41
[6] Matthew 12:40
[7] Hosea 6:2
[8] Micah 5:2
[9] I Kings 22:8, 19-23
[10] Jeremiah 26:18, 19
[11] Matthew 2:3-6
[12] II Kings 25:10
[13] Nahum 2:6
[14] Nahum 2:9
[15] Habakkuk 2:4, 5; 1:11; Daniel 4
[16] Habukkuk 2:14. The other passages are Numbers 14:21; Psalm 72:19; Isaiah 6:3; 11:9.

FOR REVIEW AND DISCUSSION

1. Give two reasons why Jonah tried to conceal his message.
2. Of what significance is Christ's reference to Jonah's experience?
3. What great prophecy did Micah make concerning the Lord Jesus?
4. Compare the prophecies and times of Nahum and Jonah.
5. What New Testament books quote Habakkuk 2:4, "The just shall live by faith"?

FOR ADDITIONAL ENRICHMENT

IRONSIDE, H. A. *The Minor Prophets.* New York: Loizeaux Bros., 1909, 8th prtg. 1963.

LAETSCH, THEO. *Bible Commentary on the Minor Prophets.* St. Louis: Concordia Pub. House, 1956.

MORGAN, G. CAMPELL. *The Minor Prophets: The Men and Their Messages.* Westwood, N.J.: Fleming H. Revell Co., 1960.

ROBINSON, GEORGE L. *The Twelve Minor Prophets.* Grand Rapids: Baker Book House, 1955.

SLEMMING, C. W. *The Bible Digest* (The Minor Prophets). Grand Rapids: Kregel Publications, 1968.

ZEPHANIAH, HAGGAI, ZECHARIAH, MALACHI

12

International changes of great importance for the kingdom of Judah occurred around 600 B.C. The great Assyrian Empire which had extended its military control to distant Thebes, 500 miles up the Nile River, disintegrated with the fall of Nineveh in 612 B.C. Babylonia, the new world power, eventually conquered Judah with the destruction of Jerusalem in 586 B.C.

Zephaniah — The Prophecy of Desolation

Zephaniah's prophecies apply to all nations. It has well been said, "If any person desires to see all the secret oracles of the Old Testament prophets reduced to one short summary, he has only to read the book of Zephaniah."

Zephaniah was active probably during the early years of Josiah's reign. Josiah at the age of eight was suddenly placed on the Davidic throne in Jerusalem in 640 B.C. He soon began to seek after God and initiated religious reforms. Assyrian influence diminished with the death of Ashurbanipal in 633 B.C., so Josiah feared no foreign interference as he attempted to rid Judah of idolatry and foreign cult worship.

Israel's tragic end had a sobering effect on Judah during the reign of Hezekiah only. Under Manasseh and Amon the sins of Judah were boundless, and when Josiah came to the throne, the kingdom was in a state of moral and spiritual degeneracy. Josiah's great reforms had not started when Zephaniah began his ministry, so his message must have encouraged the king and aroused the people to repentance. The state of moral degeneracy and indifference is evidenced by such expressions as, "Her princes within her are roaring lions; her judges are evening wolves . . . her prophets are light and treacherous persons; her priests have polluted the sanctuary, they have done violence to the law."[1]

IMPENDING DOOM (Chapter 1)

The first chapter portrays the desolation into which Judah would be plunged because of idolatrous practices in worshiping Baal and "the host of heaven upon the housetop." Josiah had destroyed idolatry outwardly, but the people cleaved to it inwardly. Black-robed priests of Baal fellowshiped with the priests of God. The wrath of God was to be poured out upon wicked men. It was popular to profess and practice the fundamental unity of all religions and to make the religion of the Scriptures complementary to the others.

JUDGMENT OF THE NATIONS (Chapters 2:1 — 3:8)

The second chapter predicts judgments upon the Philistines, the Moabites, the Ammonites, and the Ethiopians, describing accurately the desolation of Nineveh. Compare the precise predictions of Zephaniah, Amos, and Zechariah concerning the destinies of the chief cities of Philistia.[2] God's pronouncements were fulfilled; Philistia was destroyed never to rise again. The prophecy concerning the land being uninhabited has reference to the extinction of the Philistines. This is supported by the prediction that all their land would become the possession of the Jews; which prediction was fulfilled when the Jews, the remnant of the house of Judah, returned from Babylon. Since this was part of the land promised Israel under the Abrahamic Covenant,[3] it is clear that the territory was not to remain uninhabited permanently.

In the third chapter, the prophet arraigned Jerusalem and rebuked her sins. He argued that the total destruction of the neighboring nations should have caused Jerusalem to repent. But the city of David refused to learn the lesson and became more corrupt, so that it became necessary for God to cut her off.

FUTURE RESTORATION AND BLESSING (Chapter 3:9-20)

The prophecy closed with the promise of future restoration for the chosen people. They would be saved, gathered, and restored to

Palestine. In that day "the remnant of Israel shall not do iniquity," and in consequence it will be a day of rejoicing, for "the Lord hath taken away thy judgments." All that afflicted them would be punished.

Haggai — The Prophecy of the Second Temple

The prophets of the Assyrian period predicted the downfall of Samaria which took place in 722 B.C. Those of the Chaldean period predicted the destruction of Jerusalem in 586 B.C. Ezekiel, Daniel, and Obadiah prophesied during the period of the captivity. Haggai, Zechariah, and Malachi were post-exilic prophets who labored after a remnant of the Jews had been restored to their native land.

Cyrus, the Medo-Persian king, issued a decree in 536 B.C. giving the people liberty and assistance to return to their own land.[4] This concluded the seventy years of exile predicted by Jeremiah.[5] Before this decree, Cyrus had conquered Babylon and the first world power had given way to the Medo-Persian dominion.

TEMPLE CONSTRUCTION (Chapter 1)

Haggai was among the first exiles returned under Zerubbabel, the governor, and under Joshua, the high priest.[6] With his companions, he began to restore the city and rebuild the Temple. But they were soon stopped by the hostile Samaritans, who were envious of the special privilege King Cyrus had granted them. This powerful and persistent opposition lasted until 521 B.C. During this interim, the discouraged people became engrossed with their own affairs. They built paneled houses, but had no time nor money for the house of God. They complained about financial depression, and gave that as an excuse for their neglect. They continued to hope for better times, which never came. At this point, Haggai uttered his first prophecy. He urged the people to put first things first, promising that if they would obey God and rebuild the Temple, material and spiritual blessings would follow.

His words had the desired effect and the rebuilding was resumed, even though the outlook was not bright. The people were few, probably about one percent of those who constructed the first Temple. They had little means to purchase material and were unskilled in the use of it.

TEMPLE CONSOLATION (Chapter 2:1-9)

Because they had lived so long without the Temple, they felt little need of it. Haggai had to give them further, strong encouragement.

In his second prophecy, he assured them that the glory of the latter Temple should be greater than that of the first. This could hardly be understood by those who remembered Solomon's magnificent structure. Undoubtedly Haggai looked ahead to the millennial Temple[7] when the "desire of all nations" shall reign in Jerusalem.

TEMPLE SANCTITY (Chapter 2:10-19)

Three months passed with no better material prospects. For a third time the prophet encouraged the people. He rebuked their listlessness. He reminded them that as long as they were disobedient and self-willed, even their sacrifices were profane and unacceptable to God. He assured them that from the day that they would begin in earnest to restore the Temple, the plagues of mildew and hail would cease and prosperous crops would be assured.

TEMPLE POWER (Chapter 2:20-23)

The last message was spoken to Zerubbabel, the governor. Zerubbabel was a prince of the royal family of David, and the person through whom the genealogy of the Messiah can be traced in both Matthew 1 and Luke 3. God shall overthrow the thrones of kingdoms and destroy the strength of nations, but His chosen people shall be preserved and the royal family of David shall have a member to sit upon the throne of Israel. The signet ring was a token of delegated authority,[8] and Zerubbabel is here regarded as a representative or a type of Christ.

Haggai's prophecies were all pronounced within a four-month period, the exact date being given in each instance. His message concerning the shaking of the heavens and earth as well as the nations is quoted in Hebrews 12, and has reference to the physical and political upheaval that shall take place prior to the Second Coming of Christ.

Zechariah — Prophecies of the Messianic Kingdom

Zechariah was a contemporary of Haggai and served in a similar capacity to arouse the Jews to complete the Temple. A comparison of the two books will show that Zechariah confirmed the words of

Haggai and gave the weak and insignificant remnant a picture of the greater and grander restoration that would take place many centuries later. The principle of these two parallels runs through the entire Old Testament. Haggai's ministry was concerned with the Temple and the religious life of the people. Zechariah's message dealt with the nation and its political life.

A CALL TO REPENTANCE (Chapter 1:1-6)

Zechariah, like Haggai, dated his prophecies. His first message was uttered two months after the first prophecy of Haggai, while his last date is two months later than Haggai's last prophecy. "Thus saith the Lord" is found 1,904 times in the Old Testament. Zechariah used this phrase or its equivalent at least 89 times, which is one evidence that his message was inspired. "The Lord of hosts," another favorite phrase, is found 36 times and appears early in the book in Zechariah's call to repentance — "Turn ye unto me, saith the Lord of hosts, and I will turn unto you."

VISIONS OF ZECHARIAH (Chapters 1:7 — 6:8)

The book presents eight visions. The first of these symbolic visions, the man among the myrtle trees, is a picture of God's watchful care over Israel in this present age. While "the earth sitteth still, and is at rest" and "the heathen are at ease," after seventy years of exile the Jews are still molested; but God has not forgotten His people and "shall yet comfort Zion, and shall yet choose Jerusalem."

In the second symbolic vision the four horns represent the four world empires which have scattered Israel, and the four carpenters, the corresponding powers which shall eventually overcome Babylon, Persia, Greece, and Rome.

The measuring rod of the third vision symbolizes a greater Jerusalem with a vast population and whose suburbs shall extend far beyond its walls. Jeremiah also called attention to this enlarged metropolis with remarkable detail.[9] The landmarks have been definitely located and the city has already extended its borders to these points and thus fulfilled these prophecies. The future Jerusalem, instead of trusting in the security of its walls, will repose in the protection of its God.

The fourth vision records the acquittal and restoration of the priesthood through Joshua. The removal of the high priest's filthy garments symbolizes the cleansing of Israel preparatory to future service for Christ. The absence of David's throne had discouraged the returned remnant, but the prophet comforts Israel with the prediction that the Branch of David shall yet sit upon the throne.

The vision of the candlestick represents Israel, filled with the Holy Spirit, enlightening the world. The two anointed ones are Zerubbabel and Joshua, who "not by might, nor by power, but by my Spirit" will overcome all opposition and successfully complete the construction of the Temple.

The sixth vision, the flying roll, reveals the swift judgments that are to fall on individual sinners, especially thieves and perjurers.

The seventh vision, the ephah in the land of Shinar, suggests a revival of Babylon as the commercial center of the world. Babylon is recognized as the cradle of civilization. Even today it is the geographical center of the three most populous continents, Asia, Africa, and Europe. Alexander, Caesar, and Napoleon planned for its rebuilding.

The last vision, the four chariots, compares with the first vision. It represents the administration of justice throughout the world when Christ is crowned King. The chariots and horses are instruments of divine judgment.

AN OBJECT LESSON (Chapter 6:9-15)

Following the eight visions, Zechariah provides a visual object lesson. He is commanded to place crowns of silver and gold on the head of Joshua, the high priest. These represented the union of the priestly and kingly offices in the Messiah, by whom the true Temple of God would be consummated.

INSTRUCTION CONCERNING FASTS (Chapters 7, 8)

The four messages of the second portion of the book were spoken to the delegates from Babylon. They had asked whether the Lord had sanctioned the new fasts instituted during the captivity, because of the destruction of the city and the Temple. The prophet replied that God had not sanctioned such formalism and hypocrisies, but that He did require obedience to the Law and attention to the prophets' exhortations. The last two messages contain predictions of the prosperity restored in the latter days. The fasting seasons will then become cheerful feasts and the Jews will be a universal blessing.

PROPHECIES REGARDING A UNIVERSAL RULER (Chapters 9 — 14)

In the last portion of the book Zechariah presents two burdens. The first concerns the *oppressor*. The Grecian oppression is described and the Roman period culminates in the rejection of Messiah by the Jews.

The second burden concerns the *oppressed*. This depicts events that are still future and is a series of prophecies beginning with the Gentile nations laying siege to Jerusalem and being repulsed. The Jews shall mourn for their sins; a fountain will be opened for sin and uncleanness; idolatry shall be no more; and the voice of the false prophet shall cease.

The last chapter pictures Christ leading His triumphant army against the nations and ascending David's throne at Jerusalem to be King over all the earth. "Then shall the Lord go forth, and fight against those nations, as when He fought in the day of battle. And His feet shall stand in that day upon the Mount of Olives."

Finally, the prophet sees Jerusalem as the capital of the nations. Those who are "left of all the nations which came against Jerusalem shall even go up from year to year to worship the King . . . and to keep the feast." With the exception of the Psalms, the book of Zechariah contains more prophecies specifically concerning the crucifixion of Christ than any other Old Testament book. Events predicted include Christ's triumphal entry into Jerusalem; the betrayal for thirty pieces of silver; the disposal of the blood money for the potter's field; the treachery of His supposed friends; and the scattering of the disciples.[10] The New Testament lists the fulfillment of these prophecies.

Malachi — The Herald of the Messiah

Malachi, a contemporary of Nehemiah, prophesied between the second and third administration of the governor of Jerusalem. This is inferred because the Temple was evidently in existence at that time, and the evils condemned by Nehemiah were also rebuked by this prophet.

Malachi was a teacher and debater, not a poet and orator. He depended largely on argument and expostulation to arouse his hearers and to prove his assertions.

NATIONAL SINS (Chapters 1, 2)

After the people, in response to the exhortation of Haggai and Zechariah, had rebuilt the Temple, their worship became increasingly formal and selfish. Malachi enumerated five national sins about which the people were careless and unconcerned.

The first, and perhaps the most grievous of these offenses was *ingratitude*. This evil was closely related to *irreverence*. The priests were the leaders in this iniquity, but their guilt was shared by the people who followed them.

The third offence was the *unworthy priesthood*. While Zerubbabel lived, the priesthood was consecrated. Later it fell into the hands of men who were too weak to resist new temptations. The priest's office became base, contemptible, and corrupt.

The fourth iniquity was *unfaithfulness*. The people were untrue to God and to one another. "Judah hath profaned the holiness of the Lord, which He loved, and hath married the daughter of a foreign god."

The fifth sin was the *spirit of complaint*. God's people professed to serve Him, but they complained bitterly against His supposed favoritism toward the wicked. They imagined that evildoers were happy, and even when they fell into a snare, they were delivered by the Almighty. Pharisaical selfishness, so conspicuous in Christ's time, made the people utterly unconscious of the faults for which they were rebuked. Impudently and arrogantly, they repeatedly denied the charges brought against them.

JUDGMENT AND EXHORTATION (Chapters 3, 4)

In the third chapter announcement is made of the coming of John the Baptist who "shall prepare the way before" the Lord. The people were upbraided for their selfishness and were reminded of the blessing that would follow their sincere liberality in tithes and offerings.

In the closing chapter, Malachi speaks of judgment and salvation. He predicts the return of Elijah before the coming of the great and dreadful day of the Lord. Our Lord indicated that John the Baptist could have fulfilled this prophecy *if* he would have been received. However, like the One whom he announced, he was rejected. Our Lord declared after John's death that Elijah would come and restore all things. Therefore, this prophecy of the coming of Elijah must yet be fulfilled. Some believe that Elijah will be one of the two witnesses who will appear during the tribulation.[11]

As the last verse of Genesis speaks of a coffin, the last word of Malachi is the curse that followed an unfaithful and disobedient people. The entire Old Testament is the tragic story of man's failure against which the reiterated promises of a coming Redeemer appear like the rays of dawn in the blackness of night. In the New Testament we see the fulfillment of the prophecy, "the Sun of righteousness [shall] arise with healing in His wings."

NOTES

[1] Zephaniah 3:3, 4
[2] Zephaniah 2:4; Amos 1:6-8; Zechariah 9:5
[3] Genesis 15:18-21; 17:8
[4] Ezra 1:1-4
[5] Jeremiah 25:11
[6] Ezra 3:8; Haggai 1:1
[7] Ezekiel 40 — 48
[8] Genesis 41:42; Esther 3:10
[9] Jeremiah 31:38-41
[10] Zechariah 9:9; 11:12; 11:13; 13:6; 13:7
[11] Cf. Malachi 4:2, 5; Matthew 11:14; Matthew 17:11; Revelation 11

FOR REVIEW AND DISCUSSION

1. Why is the book of Zephaniah spoken of as a summary of prophecy?
2. Compare the prophecies of Haggai and Zechariah.
3. What proof is there that Malachi was a contemporary of Nehemiah?
4. With what five national sins did Malachi charge the people?
5. How do Old Testament events lead up to New Testament events?

FOR ADDITIONAL ENRICHMENT

See chapter 11, p. 83.

Date	NORTHERN KINGDOM (Israel)		SOUTHERN KINGDOM (Judah)		FOREIGN KINGS
	Kings	Writing Prophets	Writing Prophets	Kings	
931	Jeroboam Dynasty Jeroboam Nadab			Rehoboam Abijam Asa	Rezon[1]
909	Baasha Dynasty Baasha Elah Zimri (7 days)				
885	Omri Dynasty Omri (Tibni) Ahab Ahaziah Joram			Jehoshaphat Jehoram Ahaziah	Benhadad[1] Shalmaneser II[2]
841	Jehu Dynasty Jehu Jehoahaz Jehoash Jeroboam II Zechariah	Jonah Amos Hosea	Joel* Joel*	Athaliah Joash Amaziah Azariah	Hazael[1] Benhadad II[1]
752	Last Kings Shallum Menahem Pekahiah Pekah Hoshea		Isaiah	Jotham Ahaz	Tiglath-pileser III[2] Rezin[1] Shalmaneser V[2]
722	FALL OF SAMARIA		Micah Nahum*	Hezekiah Manasseh Amon	Sargon II[2] Sennacherib[2] Esarhaddon[2] Ashurbanipal[2]
640			Zephaniah* Jeremiah Habakkuk* Daniel Ezekiel	Josiah Johoahaz Jehoiakim Jehoiachin Zedekiah	Nabopolassar[3] Nebuchadnezzar[3]
586	FALL OF JERUSALEM				

Obadiah*, Haggai, Zechariah, and Malachi ministered after the Fall of Jerusalem.

* Approximate time
[1] Syria   [2] Assyria   [3] Babylonia

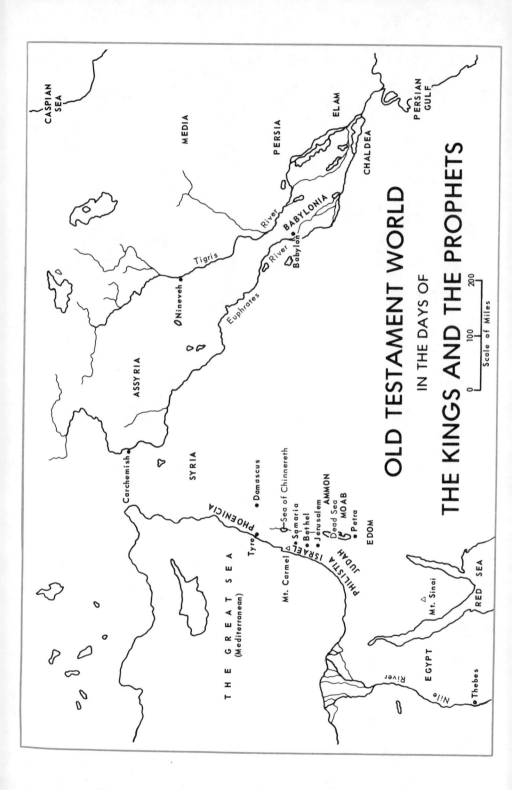

OLD TESTAMENT WORLD
IN THE DAYS OF
THE KINGS AND THE PROPHETS

Concerning E.T.T.A.

Since 1930 Evangelical Teacher Training Association has been used of God to strengthen and advance evangelical Christian education. E.T.T.A. pioneered in and continues to produce Bible-centered, Christ-honoring leadership preparation materials. These are planned to preserve and propagate the rich Gospel *message* through good educational *methods*.

Christian education is presented as an important factor in the fulfillment of Christ's commission: "Go ye therefore, and teach all nations . . . *teaching* them to observe all things, whatsoever I have commanded you" (Matt. 28:19, 20). In order to minister broadly in the advancement of Christian education, E.T.T.A. functions on three educational levels, each of which complements the others.

THE PRELIMINARY CERTIFICATE PROGRAM

Designed for local church and community leadership preparation classes this program leads to successful teaching for Sunday school teachers and officers. Six vital and challenging subjects are covered — three on Bible Survey and three on Christian Education.

Bible Survey These practical Bible Survey studies are foundational. They show the marvelous unity of the 66 books of the Bible and help one to grasp the central teaching that binds books, chapters, and verses together.

OLD TESTAMENT SURVEY — LAW AND HISTORY
A study of the books of Genesis through Esther giving an overview of God's working among men from creation through the early days of His chosen people.

OLD TESTAMENT SURVEY — POETRY AND PROPHECY
The thrilling messages of the books of Job through Malachi.

NEW TESTAMENT SURVEY
A skillful weaving of the contents of the New Testament books around the central theme — the Person of Christ.

Christian Education These subjects give insight into the pupil's personality problems, ambitions, and needs; give the "know-how" of teaching; present the overall purpose, organization, and program of the Sunday school.

UNDERSTANDING PEOPLE
This study gives insight into pupils' personalities, problems, experiences, interests, and needs.

UNDERSTANDING TEACHING or
TEACHING TECHNIQUES
Alternative texts on teaching methods which show how to communicate biblical truths and apply them to life situations.

SUNDAY SCHOOL SUCCESS
The purpose, organization, and program of the Sunday school.

An Award Credit Card is granted upon completion of each course that is taught by an instructor approved by E.T.T.A. The Preliminary Teachers Certificate is granted when the required 6 courses have been completed. A free booklet of information telling how to start E.T.T.A. classes is available.

THE ADVANCED CERTIFICATE PROGRAM

The Advanced Certificate Program gives a deep understanding of God's Word and an insight into the fields of Christian service. It is offered in E.T.T.A. affiliated Bible institutes* and is profitably presented in local church or community classes. The program consists of a minimum of 12 courses, each 12 lessons in length, and leads to the Advanced Teachers Certificate. It includes the 6 courses of the Preliminary Certificate Program and the following 6 courses.

THE MISSIONARY ENTERPRISE

This study of missions and missionary education gives vision, burden, and "know-how" for challenging new missionary outreach.

EVANGELIZE THRU CHRISTIAN EDUCATION

A challenging consideration of principles and techniques for effective soul winning in the church educational program.

THE TRIUNE GOD

The use of non-technical language makes this spiritually strengthening study of God, Christ, and the Holy Spirit helpful to all.

BIBLICAL BELIEFS

An inspiring study of salvation, inspiration of the Scriptures, the Church, angels, and last things.

CHURCH EDUCATIONAL MINISTRIES or VACATION BIBLE SCHOOL

These are alternative texts. *Church Educational Ministries* is a survey of the various educational programs which may be offered in the local church. *Vacation Bible School* is brimming with proven methods for planning, promoting, and conducting a successful vacation Bible school.

YOUR BIBLE

An enlightening presentation of the origin and authorship of the Bible, how it was preserved, and how we can answer its critics.

THE HIGHER EDUCATION PROGRAM

This specific preparation includes extensive Bible study as well as a wide selection of courses in Christian education and related subjects. It is offered only in institutions of higher education which hold Active membership in E.T.T.A.* A Diploma is awarded in recognition of required educational attainment and qualifies the holder to conduct the E.T.T.A. leadership preparation program in church or community classes.

*A list of Member Schools is available on request.